The Insider Guide to PDA

of related interest

PDA by PDAers
From Anxiety to Avoidance and Masking to Meltdowns
Sally Cat
ISBN 978 1 78592 536 8
eISBN 978 1 78450 934 7

The Parents' and Professionals' Simple Guide to PDA
Eliza Fricker and Laura Kerbey
Illustrated by Eliza Fricker
ISBN 978 1 80501 811 7
eISBN 978 1 80501 812 4

Being Julia
A Personal Account of Living with Pathological Demand Avoidance
Ruth Fidler and Julia Daunt
Foreword by Dr Judy Eaton
ISBN 978 1 84905 681 6
eISBN 978 1 78450 188 4

Navigating PDA in America
A Framework to Support Anxious, Demand-Avoidant Autistic Children, Teens and Young Adults
Ruth Fidler and Diane Gould
Foreword by Sarah C. Wayland, Ph.D.
ISBN 978 1 83997 274 4
eISBN 978 1 83997 273 7
Audio ISBN 978 1 39982 082 0

The Insider Guide to PDA

Sally Cat and
Brook Madera

Jessica Kingsley Publishers
London and Philadelphia

First published in Great Britain in 2026 by Jessica Kingsley Publishers
An imprint of John Murray Press

2

Content Warning: This book mentions addiction, depression, and suicidal ideation.

A CIP catalogue record for this title is available from the British Library and the Library of Congress

ISBN 978 1 39983 069 0
eISBN 978 1 39983 070 6

Printed and bound in the United States by Integrated Books International

Jessica Kingsley Publishers' policy is to use papers that are natural, renewable and recyclable products and made from wood grown in sustainable forests. The logging and manufacturing processes are expected to conform to the environmental regulations of the country of origin.

Jessica Kingsley Publishers
Carmelite House
50 Victoria Embankment
London EC4Y 0DZ

www.jkp.com

John Murray Press
Part of Hodder & Stoughton Ltd
An Hachette Company

The authorised representative in the EEA is Hachette Ireland,
8 Castlecourt Centre, Dublin 15, D15 XTP3, Ireland (email: info@hbgi.ie)

Contents

Foreword

I always start my training sessions with the quote below by Seth Godin, a renowned author and entrepreneur, who is best known for his work on leadership and change. It appeared in my inbox shortly after the PDA North America Annual Conference (PDANA), striking a deep chord with all that I was feeling at that moment in my life:

> In search of incompetence
>
> Learning is about becoming incompetent on our way to getting better.
>
> If you're not open to the tension that is caused by knowing you could do better, it's unlikely you're willing to do the work to get better. As you're doing that work, there's the satisfaction it brings, but also the knowledge that just a moment ago, you weren't any good.

I was formally introduced to Brook Madera's and Sally Cat's work early in 2024 as I prepared to be the keynote speaker at the PDANA Annual Conference. I was invited to speak at the event because of the distinctly positive impact my book *The Declarative Language Handbook* had on PDA families. To prepare I read a handful of recommended books and explored on-line resources related to PDA and was doing my best to learn what I could as a person outside the PDA community being invited in, to offer meaningful tools and communication strategies.

I knew what I knew quite well—declarative language, co-regulation, social learning, dynamic communication, and to prioritize the fostering of positive relationships, trust, and connection as the foundation of any clinical work. And I embraced the commitment to be a continually evolving neurodiversity-affirming clinician. This work is and has been in my heart and my soul for more than 30 years, long before I had the language to describe my values in this way. It is my passion and path in life to be a lifelong learner, to do better, to deepen relationships, to broaden the complexity and nuance of my understanding, and to share what I know with others in ways that are accessible to all. I am continually amazed and humbled to uncover new nuggets of information in this world as more neurodivergent individuals share their experiences and voices.

As I was preparing my talk, I trusted I had valuable information to share, but also wanted to get it right, and to do right by this unique community. Although comfortable in my areas of competence, I am also acutely, and sometimes painfully, aware when I *don't* know something. I quickly came to realize that those few days in Chicago were much more about me as a student than me as a teacher.

As I was immersed in the PDA community that week, I found myself surrounded by a community that was keenly insightful and knowledgeable, yet also so vulnerable and in so much pain for not being seen in the larger professional world. I had never experienced anything like it—so deep, so real, so powerful—and it moved me to my core. From that point, I set out to immerse myself further in the community, to learn from them, and to train my team back home on the topic of PDA and PDA-affirming approaches so that we all could get it right and be better.

I now consider Brook a good friend, but also an incredible teacher and mentor to me and other professionals, families, and PDAers. Her written and spoken voice is insightful, fun, funny, witty, creative, real, practical, unfiltered, and vulnerable, and her teaching is generous, kind, patient, and thoughtful. The tension around PDA learning may be real, but Brook creates a positive and safe experience for all who are willing to engage with it.

And Sally Cat, a strong, consistent, and brave voice in the PDA world, has always led the way in this area! Through her prior books, *PDA by PDAers* and *Pathological Demand Avoidance Explained*, her blog, her vivid memes, and by initiating her Big Traits study of 2016 that captured the experiences and voices of over 300 individuals, autistic and PDAers, to statistically determine what makes the PDA experience different, she shows us all how to move forward and build upon her findings and insights so that we as a community do better.

The PDA voice, when safe to express itself, is unique, nuanced, down to earth, intelligent, sensitive, practical, and real. If we let it, it guides us into what often becomes best practice for all. I am thrilled that Brook and Sally Cat have come together as authors in this book, so that we all can benefit from their knowledge, practical advice, deep understanding, experience, and compassion.

Brook's and Sally Cat's *The Insider Guide to PDA* is a holistic and comprehensive guide to all things PDA. As I read it, I found myself keeping an internal list of thoughts and questions to follow up on after having finished. Yet, inevitably, as I continued reading, I learned I didn't need to because Brook and Sally Cat covered it all! They truly left no stone unturned, no question unasked, no thought unaddressed.

If you are new to PDA, this guide will offer you a thorough understanding of PDA—the challenges across the lifespan, how to tease out what is PDA versus what is not, what you can do that will be immediately helpful, and more. It also includes a section on the wonderful and unique gifts of PDAers so these are not overlooked (a chapter that I loved!).

And, if you are already familiar with PDA, this guide will undoubtedly expand your knowledge by exploring the nooks and crannies of topics and questions you didn't yet know you had and serve as a handy guide to refer to by topic on an as-needed basis. I know I will have a few copies ready on my bookshelf as specific questions arise for myself, my colleagues, and my clients of all ages.

Brook's and Sally Cat's *Insider Guide* is easy to understand and accessible to readers of all backgrounds—one of my favorite types of resources! It provides important content, while also sharing personal experiences where you may find familiarity, and always in a voice that is easy to imagine speaking to you directly in a comfortable, intimate setting. And, for those seeking data and concrete evidence, be assured that the findings from Sally Cat's 2016 Big Traits study are discussed throughout this book. Her full findings can be found at www.sallycatpda.co.uk/2024/06/big-traits-study-results.html, and can help us all build evidence-based practice around, and acceptance of, PDA.

I am grateful for the voices in the PDA community, and especially grateful for Brook and Sally Cat. I know I am a better clinician, professional, and person because of what I have learned from them, and importantly from their embrace of me into their community. As you read this book, I think you will feel their welcome, generous embrace as well.

Linda K. Murphy
Author of *Declarative Language Handbook* and
Co-Regulation Handbook
July 2025

Introduction

Many families learning about PDA—"pathological" demand avoidance—come from a place of distress. Often, their children have been run through every kind of public support that is available, including through the education system, and they are terrified to see their children getting worse.

There is, though, a lot of conflicting information about what PDA is—and isn't. One of our aims in writing this book is to mop up this confusion by giving clear examples based on our own lived experiences as PDA adults who have PDA kids of our own, as well as our combined experiences in speaking with hundreds of families.

Traditional descriptions of PDA (what we will refer to as "externalized PDA") tell of children with loud, easy-to-spot traits, like bossing teachers around and having violent meltdowns. However, not all PDA is freely expressed (what we will refer to as "internalized PDA"), so its existence tends to go unnoticed. This is explored further in Chapter 2.

In fact, even when PDA people show distress, their internal drivers are invisible. For example, the teacher will be aware that a freely expressing PDA kid is unsettled in class and prone to lashing out at fellow pupils and staff, but the teacher won't know what is triggering their behaviors. The teacher may scratch their head and wonder if the child has conduct disorder. Or might it be oppositional defiant disorder? Attention deficit hyperactivity disorder (ADHD)? Poor parenting? Attention seeking? Possession by a devil? (See Chapter 4.)

When PDA isn't openly expressed, there is even less likelihood of it being recognized. Especially since the individual PDA person isn't being overtly disruptive. The reality, though, is that no matter how our PDA is demonstrated, our natural wiring causes us to be labeled misfits to society. With appropriate support, we can flourish. Without it, our lives car-crash into ruin.

If this sounds melodramatic, it's not. PDA really does impact us to this degree. What ignorant observers see are high school drop-outs, young people with eating disorders, petty criminals, mental breakdowns, food bank users, and other social "failures." It's just that our neurological wiring throws many hurdles in our way. With awareness and support, we can achieve great things. This is why it's so important to recognize PDA in all its forms and understand how to support it, because support put in place at an earlier stage can prevent PDA people from sinking.

It should be borne in mind that quieter expressions of PDA, which are often referred to as "internalized," aren't lesser or milder, in the same way that an iceberg isn't smaller than a same-sized block of ice sitting on dry land. It's simply the case that most of the iceberg is hidden by the seawater it's submerged in.

Many clinicians who are familiar with PDA believe it to be very rare, and that other conditions—such as autism with extreme demand avoidance and ADHD—are mistaken for PDA. However, it may well be that hidden PDA is actually quite common. It's just that only the freely expressed or "externalized" variety gets noticed. PDA is little known, and internalized PDA is lesser known still.

This book explains what PDA is and the variety of ways it can be hidden, before examining root causes behind our visible behaviors and how PDA can be effectively supported. Our aim is for this book to be both informative and readable by blending textbook-style explanations with our own first-hand accounts as PDA adults involved with the greater PDA community and who have PDA kids of our own.

A "PDA PERSON" OR A "PERSON WITH PDA"?

Another way to pose the question of whether it's preferable to say a "PDA person" or a "person with PDA" is to ask whether *person-first* or *identity-first* language should be used.

It's not our place to tell PDA people how to describe themselves to others. This section is intended first for people interacting with the PDA community, including parents who are in the process of learning about PDA. Second, we believe this information might be of interest to fellow PDA adults who've not come across it before. Third, anyone who starts interacting with the wider autism community will quickly come across this debate, and it pays to be informed of both sides.

Identity-first language

Identity-first language means saying an "X person"—for example, an autistic person.

Person-first language

Person-first language means saying a "person with X"—for example, "a child with PDA"—and is based on the belief that labels such as PDA and autism shouldn't define people because it diminishes them and takes away their wider identities. The thinking is that if identity-first language is used, and a child is referred to as integrally autistic, people will forget that they've got a personality beyond autism. A majority of professionals including diagnosticians and school staff use person-first language when talking about conditions such as autism and PDA, as they believe this to be respectful.

Another way of saying this is that it *pathologizes* them. Collins Dictionary defines "pathologize, or pathologise" as a verb meaning "to represent (something) as a disease," giving the example of, "this pathologizing of parenthood."[1] Eagle-eyed readers may have joined dots and will be thinking that if it's wrong to pathologize neurotypes, the word "pathological" in PDA's name must be problematic too. We'll address this in Chapter 1.

The problem with person-first language

As we've said, individuals have every right to refer to themselves as they wish. So if they prefer to use person-first language and call themself a person with PDA, this is entirely their right.

Beyond this, however, there's a good reason to use identity-first language by saying "PDA people." By encouraging people to think of neurotypes like autism and PDA as separate from the individuals they describe—"person *with* PDA"—person-first language gives the illusion that these are curable disorders, which in turn leaves neurodivergent children vulnerable to abusive and dramatic "cures" that are doomed to fail.

A parallel example is the now discredited belief that left-handed children should be forced to use their right hands. The practice was abandoned after it was realized that handedness is hardwired, and trying to change it is not only pointless but harmful as it caused multiple chronic neurological side-effects such as stuttering and acquired learning disabilities.[2] Attempts to force heterosexuality have largely been abandoned for similar reasons in the West. The autism community has highlighted that trying to cure or suppress autism via applied behavior analysis (ABA) "therapy" has had disastrous consequences for autistic individuals who often develop post-traumatic stress disorder (PTSD).

It is worth noting that there are intersecting communities that adopt person-first language to help them feel safer due to the myriad of other risks they maneuver on a day-to-day basis as Black, Indigenous, or otherwise people of color (BIPOC). As we attempt to make affirming strides, it's responsible to note that not every culture is in the position to defend why they adopt the language that they do, and pressing them to do so only adds emotional labor. Admittedly, while it's pretty easy to talk about "autistic people" in place of "people with autism," it's more challenging to talk about PDA people—or, for that matter, ADHD people—unless the acronym is thought of as an adjective.

Many autistic people believe that every issue they face can be explained by the "social model of disability," meaning that they are only disabled when society fails to accommodate their specific needs. It's our opinion, however, that the social model of disability doesn't account for every instance of inability that PDA people encounter, because our illogical variety of demand avoidance is internally driven and blocks us from doing things we actually want to do and that would benefit us. In this sense, we feel that our PDA defines us more than our autism. While we can happily affirm that our autism doesn't define us, our PDA does because there are always things it will stop us from doing, regardless of how many social accommodations are in place.

CHAPTER 1

What Is PDA?

PDA refers to both a type of avoidance and a neurotype (brain type). This can cause confusion because the neurotype comprises more traits than the demand avoidance it's named for.

As PDA is the name of a neurotype, the acronym can be used as an adjective ("pee-dee-ay"). So, for example, we can say, "That person is PDA." The PDA acronym can also be used as an adjective in the same way that the word "autistic" is used—for example, "I'm a PDA person."

ISN'T "PATHOLOGICAL" A DIRTY WORD?

Although the term has been criticized because "pathology" is traditionally used to describe diseases, we still feel it's the most accurate description of the severity and impact of the demand avoidance we experience. We hope to reclaim the term "pathological" for our own purposes in the same way that the term "disabled," which in times past was considered to have a negative connotation, has been reclaimed by the disability community. In the context of PDA, "pathological" indicates that our demand avoidance is biologically rooted and, as such, not caused by traumatic experiences.

For the reasons given in the introduction, our stance is that PDA individuals can use any words that they feel best fit their PDA. For us, "pathological" simply means: "It is beyond our conscious control and, sometimes, beyond our comprehension."

PDA TRAITS OVERVIEW

The PDA neurotype is characterized by a cluster of traits:

- "pathological" demand avoidance
- high anxiety
- high personal control need
- social naivety, sometimes described as shallow social understanding
- interest in people (which may become obsessive)
- fondness of novelty
- strong, changeable emotions
- role play/social creativity
- being drawn to fantasy and role play
- not bound by social hierarchy.

It's worth exploring each trait in detail to provide insider perspectives.

"Pathological" demand avoidance

Our "pathological" demand avoidance is an inborn drive to avoid anything, and everything, regardless of whether or not it would benefit us. It can be considered irrational because it's based on threats our minds have dreamt up, rather than knowledge of genuine danger.

It's the polar opposite of the well-known advertising slogan "Just do it." We can't "just do" anything because of our inbuilt resistance to doing...well, anything.

This avoidance drive can feel as nondescript as not wanting to pick up a drink that's right beside us on the table when we're thirsty, or struggling to complete a task today that we easily did yesterday just by virtue of feeling pressure to do it well "consistently." No two PDA people share exactly the same avoidances.

Other examples of PDA-type avoidance are automatically saying "no" to invitations before weighing up whether we'd enjoy the activity; never watching a film because someone recommended it; ignoring instructions and botching things as a result; and delaying paying bills when we have enough finances to pay them and are aware of the bills, but very strongly object to "having to" pay them.

Another key feature of our PDA-type avoidance is that it attaches directly to the perception of a demand. The intensity of our drive to avoid can decrease if expectations around fulfilling the demand are lessened. If it's reframed as something we don't have to do, we'll feel less pressure to avoid it.

As an example, if a loved one has told us that they really want us to go to the beach, our PDA brain is almost guaranteed to go into high avoidance alert and veto the idea. But if our loved one communicates that it's OK if we don't go too, our triggered avoidance is less.

We often don't notice we're avoiding something sometimes until we're confronted with it. This could be because society's rules have forced us to stay in a school or work environment, or we're given a court summons for an unpaid debt, or even if a well-meaning friend has kept pushing us to watch a certain film. In all cases, we can no longer quietly avoid the place/bill/film, and adrenaline and cortisol surge through us to put us into defense mode. Whether our reaction is to go into meltdown, run away, or tailspin in a semi-catatonic state, to observers our reaction seems disproportionate to the trigger.

This is why it's common for parents to report their child's PDA "appearing" when they hit a major developmental marker or after starting primary school.

It's not possible to remove all the demands a PDA person is faced with, as life is filled with demands, but it is possible to reduce their intensity so that our demand avoidance isn't triggered as strongly. This is explored in the final chapter, Effective Strategies and Interventions.

> **Sally:** My avoidance reaction doesn't feel emotional at all. It's more like a switch having silently flicked from on to off in my head, immediately killing all my desire for whatever it is that my brain's switched off from.
>
> It's only if I can't avoid something that panic sets in.
>
> I think this is an important point, because lots of people assume that PDA is a trauma response. The truth is that the triggering of my avoidance doesn't feel remotely traumatic.

Anxiety

There doesn't seem to be anything unique about the anxiety PDA people experience, but what stands out is the sheer quantity of it that we feel. For this reason, PDA anxiety can be described as "next level" because it's not your run-of-the-mill variety which afflicts most people sometimes.

Constant anxiety appears to be an integral part of PDA: a monster that's breathed down our necks since the moment our lives began. It causes us to overthink and imagine disastrous outcomes based on no real evidence.

Traditional descriptions of PDA say our avoidance is an anxiety-driven need for control. However, organizations such as PDA North America and the PDA Society no longer say this. From personal experience, we think it's misleading to view PDA avoidance as anxiety-driven because we've felt our instinct to avoid sparking before anxiety sets in. To put it another way, the stress associated with avoiding demands seems to happen when we're not able to avoid things our brain tells us to avoid.

Young or old, our anxiety may be expressed as phobias about

certain foods or things that feel beyond us to face. Examples from our own experience include:

- tomato seeds
- aphids on salad
- the number 7
- removing a Band-Aid
- going to sleep (believing it will cause death).

The social focus element of PDA can flavor our anxiety too:

- solitude
- scrutiny
- making mistakes
- ridicule
- condemnation
- suffocation from another's neediness
- rejection.

Paradoxically, we PDA people may argue a point, despite being terrified of hearing counter-arguments, and actually continue to press our point despite this terror. Similarly, PDA people of all ages may carry out outrageous acts that are designed to attract attention, but be totally panicked by any attention received, especially if it's critical.

Medication and therapy may help alleviate some of our anxiety, but our drive to avoid things seems to precede it. We discuss medicating anxiety and our cautions about giving mind-altering drugs to children in Chapter 10: Effective Strategies and Interventions.

Control need

The high control need that comes with PDA isn't about wanting to control others, but about being instinctively driven to control our personal worlds. It's easy, though, for our attempts to gain personal control to spill onto others without having wanted to control them for the sake of it.

Our need for control is fired by other people exercising their free will and doing things that run contrary to our own plans. This may cause us to behave hypocritically by, on the one hand, assuming the right to bend rules while, on the other hand, being outraged when other people bend rules too. There's a clear link between PDA control need and our "pathological" style of avoidance, because not coping with contrary plans equates with not coping with people demanding that we do things their way.

Our innate control need can cause us to automatically veto other people's ideas and organize things our own way. Harmony between PDA individuals can be hard to maintain because of our conflicting control needs, and feeling out of control tends to trigger our demand avoidance so we can't engage any more.

> **Sally:** As a young adult, I was horrified by the idea of being a control freak. This was not the type of person I wanted to be. At the same time, I couldn't cope with being out of control with things that impacted my day-to-day world. The guy who lived downstairs had kick-ass bass speakers which blasted his music right through our house. It drove me crazy, not just because of my hypersensitivity to sound, but because I was forced to hear my housemate's music. My need to control my own world superseded my painful shyness and drove me downstairs to persuade him to turn the volume down again.

Social naivety

Traditional descriptions of PDA describe us as sociable but lacking depth in our understanding. This may or may not be true for all PDA people, but it rings true for us both. Social naivety can cause us to make repeated social blunders by misconstruing what others want. What can be confusing to observers is that in some areas we can seem intensely aware of social nuance and meaning, while in other areas we can seem completely blind.

> **Sally:** I was confused during my younger years because people kept responding as if I'd made huge social errors, either by laughing at me or shunning me. No matter how hard I tried not to blunder again, I always did, though I didn't know why.
>
> Even my family and best friend treated me as if I was intensely stupid, which confused me massively.

Fortunately, we PDA people are often able to be very charming and can use this to win people over. This is an extremely helpful counterbalance to our social blundering.

Conversely, other PDA traits may cause other people to feel ill at ease. For example, many PDA individuals have quirky senses of humor, often pushing boundaries for fun. We've learned to suppress this after realizing it upsets others and drives them away. It may seem obvious that provoking people will annoy them, but PDA brains sometimes struggle to foresee the consequences.

> **Brook:** One of my kids will pick up on crude, morbid, and child-inappropriate phrases so that I am frequently redirecting and enlightening him on the deeper meanings. Paradoxically, this same child squirms and chastises me for socially acceptable terms of affection such as me stating that he is handsome, or reminding him that he used to say he wanted to marry me.

Another potentially annoying PDA trait that we've noticed is having a penchant for giving unsolicited nicknames that aren't always welcomed by their recipient. Wordplay is explored in more depth in Chapter 5: PDA Positives.

> **Brook:** In our house of (at least four) PDA people, we are constantly nicknaming our pets. We have one cat in particular, affectionately named "Beans," who is rotating through variations of "Beanie baby," "Bens," "Bees," and, recently, "The Bean's Knees."

Social focus (which may become obsessive)

Being socially focused means that other people factor in our thoughts. It causes us to be interested in what others think and how they interact with each other, and with us. It makes us want to engage with other people. We may desperately want to have friends but lack crucial social skills to achieve this. For example, we boss our friends around, or are too tongue-tied with anxiety to forge social bonds.

Social focus may also impact PDA people's choice of special interests. A clichéd example of an autistic special interest is trainspotting, but the range of special interests is far wider than this and includes animals, characters from comics or TV shows, hobbies, and music. PDA brains, however, have a tendency to fixate on particular people, and this can happen to an all-consuming degree.

PDA people's intense obsessions about others can be positive or negative. If the obsession is positive, the technical term is "limerence." Limerence causes us to see the person we're fixated on as unrealistically perfect. It's an unpleasant state to be stuck in and can feel impossible to escape from. PDA people may also develop negative obsessions, whereby they view another person as a threat and, sometimes, target them for abuse. See also scapegoating in Chapter 9.

We believe that the social focus element of our PDA is so strong that the inner workings of our neurotype can't be understood without it being factored in. Our social focus is as fundamental and unstoppable as our brain's drive to avoid, and means that our avoidance strategies incorporate social awareness.

> **Brook:** My intense focus on people started as a young adult with my "crushes." I didn't feel safe getting emotionally close to others, in part because of my childhood trauma, but in large part because I didn't instinctively understand how to get close to people in a way that felt like I wasn't somehow losing control of myself.

Fondness of novelty

Novelty presents us with a wonderfully fresh vista in which our brains haven't yet detected any nasty demands to panic about and tell us to avoid.

While most autistic people seem to prefer routines that they've consented to,[1] PDA individuals can find routines triggering, regardless of whether or not they had a say in establishing them. That's not to say that we hate all routines, especially ones that we've created for ourselves. An example of this would be having developed a particular order of doing things after we wake up (toilet, brush teeth, kettle, drink coffee, check email, or something else). In fact, routines enable us to bypass our brain's constant stream of demands that it wants us to avoid, by lumping tasks into a familiar process, such as washing the dishes. Our brain will still object, but have fewer separate activities to object to.

Novelty is the antithesis of routine. It's an untrodden path glittering with possibilities, as opposed to the well-worn circuit of a familiar routine. Although it should be borne in mind that no two autistic people are the same, love of novelty, like social focus, marks PDA as a condition that's distinct from autism as it's generally understood.

> **Brook:** It always makes me anxious to have someone else tell me where we're going to eat, but I do like trying new things, so my instinct is to always respond with somewhere else I've never gone before. This has generated hurt feelings in my close friends and family who didn't understand how instantly unappealing a place was as soon as they said it, but how trying somewhere "new" was a way for me to make the demand of their request bearable.

Strong, changeable emotions, including meltdowns

PDA people's emotions may have a tendency to plummet from high to low, then back again, at great speed, as if riding a roller coaster.

Parents of PDA kids often describe them having Jekyll and Hyde personalities: being calm and happy, then, suddenly, exploding into rage but quickly calming down again.

The word "meltdown" is often used to describe an episode of anger, but this isn't the true meaning of the term. Melting down is closer to a feeling of overwhelm and it may not even express itself as anger. It's an uncontrollable response to our brains overloading so much that they can no longer function, and has been likened to an emotional epileptic fit. It is as frightening for us as it is for those who observe us. Overloading can be caused by sensory bombardment, imposed changes, or escalating anxiety. PDA children are especially prone to melting down because of their high anxiety and control needs.

> **Brook:** My meltdown starts with me getting more and more robotic, emotionless. I try to control my stressors as much as possible. As that fails, then my emotions break through, usually as irritability and anger with someone I trust, or as crying if I'm unlucky to have it happen around a stranger.

Using creative and/or social strategies to avoid demands

A much-touted textbook example of using a creative, social strategy to avoid a demand is a child saying "My legs don't work" in response to them having been asked to walk somewhere. Another example is a child going out during a bitterly cold winter storm without wearing a coat, and claiming that all coats are too heavy.

In both cases, inventive social negotiation is used to justify avoidance, in place of blunt, outright refusal. These social strategies may give the impression that our needs are arbitrary, but we may lean on them, sometimes without conscious awareness, to conceal the anxiety triggered by the requests.

> **Sally:** I find myself giving ridiculous excuses to my pets, who, obviously, can't understand the nonsense I'm telling them anyway. The kind of fantastical excuses I say to them is "I can't get you more food now because my head is falling off and, if I move,

> it will roll across the floor and then we'll all be in trouble, so I can't get to your food. Sorry." I don't know where these words come from. Well, from my PDA brain, I guess. It makes me laugh.

Being drawn to fantasy and role play

Traditional descriptions of PDA say that people, young and old, are drawn to fantasy and/or role play. Being drawn to fantasy means being prone to daydreaming or, in other ways, creating a model of the world that's based on their own imagination, as opposed to objective reality. Fantasy can soothe the pain of control loss and other stresses, such as high anxiety, that PDA people are susceptible to.

Role play refers to adopting a persona or alter ego. This could be a toddler deciding that they're Peter Rabbit, or an adult imagining that they're being filmed for YouTube while they carry out a task. Role play can bypass demand avoidance by making demands feel novel.

> **Sally:** When we booked a holiday to Morocco a few years ago, I was excited to research how best to dress and behave as a female visitor. I packed long, loose-fitting skirts and tops, and hats for my head. When we were there, I found it immensely pleasurable to assume the role of a submissive female and, donned in my body-hiding garb, walk a few paces behind my partner with my head bowed low. I loved the feeling of my floor-length skirt swooshing against my legs as I walked. The novelty was exhilarating.

Disregard for social hierarchy

We PDA people have a tendency to resist power imbalances that require us to cede control to others. While all this is going on inside, we might be simultaneously aware that disrespecting established hierarchies will reflect poorly on us. It should, though, be borne in mind that, like everyone else, PDA people have prejudices from their upbringings and so may not treat people purely on their own merit.

Further, if a PDA person believes an existing social structure protects their autonomy, they may actively enforce it without considering if doing this will help or hinder others.

> **Brook:** I absolutely have never believed anyone in any position to be "better" than me in a way that I have seen peers reflect, but this only made me terrified around those who had authority over me. The reality that I perceived life differently made me feel vulnerable to what I felt were arbitrary behaviors of people who could hurt me with their decisions. Not only that, but because they didn't see me as an equal I felt like I had no real way to defend myself.

WHY THE TRADITIONAL LIST OF PDA TRAITS ISN'T EXHAUSTIVE

The traits we've so far looked at were identified by PDA's pioneering theorist Professor Elizabeth Newson and her team, which included Phil Christie, who has authored several books about PDA. Vital as their work has been for illuminating the existence of PDA, understanding of all neurodiversity is still very much a work in progress. There's no concrete knowledge about what any neurodivergent condition is, or isn't.

In the interim, lived experiences can, and do, provide windows into the inner workings of PDA, as well as other neurodivergent conditions.

CHAPTER 2

How PDA Is Hidden

ALL PDA IS HIDDEN

It's important to be aware that all PDA is hidden because, no matter how freely it is expressed, its inner drivers are invisible to observers. This means that no end of guesswork and assumption-making takes place as people try to make sense of the behavior of a PDA child or adult.

Internalized PDA

Although traditional descriptions of PDA describe only the externalized, freely expressed variety, this isn't because internalized PDA doesn't exist, but because clinicians and theorists didn't notice this quieter presentation. Internalized PDA is exactly the same as the type of PDA that's described in textbooks and traits lists, except our strong emotions and meltdowns are contained and masked.

The concept of internalized PDA has been steadily gaining attention because it rings true for parents and others who've found that the traditional (externalized) description of PDA doesn't quite fit their child, themselves, or some other person they're seeking to make sense of. When PDA is internalized, our roller-coasting emotions and also our meltdowns are contained inside us, almost as if we swallow them to stop them getting away from us. Instead of screaming and crying when hurt, we may remain silent but betray our internalized stress in some other, disconnected manner. For example, we may become oddly rigid or put on a false smile.

Hiding our meltdowns and wild emotional swings may confuse observers who've picked up on our high tension but been confronted with our external calmness. This can make them feel uncomfortable because the subtle signals they detected mismatch our body language.

Things become extra uncomfortable and confusing when we melt down. Because they're contained, internalized meltdowns are expressed in splutteringly brittle ways as if we've got a firework in our stomach. In place of smashing things up or yelling, we may fiercely nitpick or take ourselves away and self-harm. This is similar to what the medical field terms "referred pain"—pain that doesn't obviously link to the body part that's causing it, such as a pain in the jaw for a heart attack. In this same way, PDA behaviors don't always directly link to the thing that triggered them.

Some people's PDA is variable, meaning it's a mixture of internalized and externalized. This can happen if someone who usually internalizes their anger suddenly blasts it out when a person they care about is being threatened.

> **Sally:** I automatically try to contain any strong emotions that well up inside me. They feel threatening and I'm scared to let them run freely.

Externalized PDA

It may seem odd to include externalized PDA in this section, but its inner workings are just as hidden from observers as its internalized counterpart.

Even if PDA has been diagnosed, external expressions of PDA can be assumed to be the byproduct of other factors, which are not its real roots. Kids who kick into "fight" can be presumed not to care about the damage they're causing. Flight and other adrenal responses are explored in more detail in Chapter 3.

When reading stories of families in distress, it's common to come across externalized expressions of PDA being mistaken for defiance, arrogance, or poor character. We explore parent blaming in Chapter 4.

> **Sally:** I recklessly ran down our street shouting and seeking out gunmen after my housemate told me some guys had demanded money from him at gunpoint.

Unmeant accusations during meltdown

Regardless of whether we internalize or externalize, when we melt down, we're not in control of what we say and do, even if we yell at our loved ones or smash things up. This can confuse and distress anyone in the vicinity of a PDA meltdown because they've assumed all the foul words and violent behaviors are meant genuinely and that the melting-down individual seriously hates them.

Confusion such as this can make already stressed family dynamics even worse because the parent or other caregiver assumes the child needs discipline and punishment for having behaved with violence. But neither discipline nor punishment will take away the underlying super-stress that caused the meltdown to happen, and parental shame, anger, and pressure only add fuel to the internal fire. We explore techniques for soothing and avoiding meltdowns in Chapter 10.

> **Sally:** I hate being in meltdown. It's like being possessed by an evil demon that has access to every scrap of my knowledge about the people I'm with, so it can make me say the cruelest possible things to hurt them. I witness my nastiness in mute horror. I feel so ashamed and hate myself.

Emotion blindness

The very fact that our anxiety has always been with us means that we may not spot it. This is because we don't know any difference, as it's the only state of being that we know. Additionally, many PDA people report being alexithymic, meaning we're unable to read our own emotions. We are detached from the roller-coasting feelings that are constantly whooshing up, down, and all around inside us.

> **Sally:** A doctor once offered me a paper bag to breathe into because I was having a panic attack. I'd not even noticed!

Atypical adrenal responses

PDA anxiety and control need make our adrenal glands prone to being triggered to release the stress hormones of adrenaline and cortisol. Most people are familiar with the adrenal trio of fight, flight, and freeze, but we believe there are other lesser-known adrenal responses. These include fawning, fantasizing, fooling around (a.k.a. funster), and fibbing. If our adrenal reactions are diverted from fight or flight into lesser-known responses, this may give the impression that we're lazy or naughty, whereas, in fact, enormous stress drives us.

Another atypical dimension of PDA in terms of adrenal responses is how "trigger prone" we are. Polyvagal theory accounts for some of this. Atypical adrenal reactions are explored in greater detail in Chapter 3.

> **Brook:** I can be very engaging, social, and charming. I was in public speaking and drama, and I loved teaching people about a special interest if they seemed remotely interested.
>
> But the dark side was when I felt stressed in a social situation; I turned dominating by debating any ideas I felt were

> under threat, and I sometimes also made awkward, inappropriate jokes. I always felt ashamed afterwards, but in the moment I felt terrified and confused about how to act.

Invisible demand avoidance

As we saw in the previous chapter, our "pathological" variety of demand avoidance only tends to show up when we can't avoid the object or activity that our brain wants us to avoid. When this happens, our adrenal glands flood our systems with adrenaline and cortisol, causing us to react in a variety of ways that can mystify observers.

Additionally, as for our anxiety, our demand avoidance is as natural as breathing, and we tend not to notice it.

> **Brook:** I avoided demands without noticing until I got married. Then, once I had someone in my life who had opinions on what we did, and kids who needed me in ways I couldn't escape, I could see how much it depleted me to not have flexibility.
>
> Now that my life is simpler with more support, I see how essential it is for me to have choices of things to do or not do, so that I can listen to my PDA when it whispers "No."

Quibbling

Our PDA control need can cause children to argue like little lawyers, passionately quibbling about random cases of their own invention. This lawyer-like quibbling is sparked by feeling out of control, which is unendurable to PDA brains, and is an attempt to regain the necessary feeling of control by persuading parents, or others, to agree with them on all counts. If a parent accepts their child's argument that black is white, or some other equally improbable thing, the child regains that vital sense of having personal control that comes with their PDA.

Internalized meltdowns can show on the surface as manic and highly irrational quibbling—for example, insisting that all people deserve the right to lie on wet lawns after dark, or that 2 + 2 = 5 because the plus sign needs to be counted along with the 2s. If this happens, it can be best not to argue and remain calm until the child's brittle argumentativeness subsides.

> **Brook:** I was the little lawyer growing up. If anyone stated any idea definitively, my instinct was to counter their point of view in order to find balance. The idea of being trapped by ideas was threatening to me, though I didn't know it at the time.

Passive early years

Being quiet during babyhood and preschool years is a form of obviously hidden PDA that's made it into established traits lists. We take a close look at infant passivity in Chapter 6: Babyhood and Toddlerhood.

> **Brook:** Unless I had a best friend to talk to, I was a very quiet kid. I didn't make waves, or have strong opinions. I read my favorite books or drew pictures. It wasn't until middle school that I felt comfortable enough in my own skin to crack a joke in front of my peers, and I remember a boy looked at me, shocked, and said, "I didn't know you were funny!"

MASKING

"Masking" has become a dirty word within the autism community. Masking is thought of as harmful and unnatural. However, we believe there are at least four different types of masking, of which only one is the harmful type. Although all four masking types look similar externally, they're caused by markedly different internal processes.

Sally Cat, in 2018, was the first person to propose that some forms of masking have positive benefits for neurodivergent people, and that unforced masking may be particularly common within the PDA population. It's important to differentiate between types of masking so that their different processes are understood and, as appropriate, avoided, accommodated, or utilized.

Directly imposed masking

This is the highly damaging form of masking that the autism community has in mind when they say masking can and should be dropped. Imposed masking involves suppressing natural neurodivergent traits, regardless of the cost to the individual, because someone else demands it.

Forced masking is a key feature of applied behavior analysis (ABA) "therapy," which autistic children are frequently subjected to. It is especially common in the United States. ABA uses the same basic methods that an experimental neurologist, named Pavlov, pioneered to program dogs to drool whenever he rang a bell. Similarly, children subjected to ABA are conditioned to make eye contact and to suppress hand flapping, spinning, and other physical actions that are necessary for them to self-regulate.

The resulting trauma of ABA has been shown to cause post-traumatic stress disorder.[1]

> **Brook:** An anonymous member of our PDA community has shared how ABA only hurt him, and didn't help him learn any new skills. He shared that anything ABA therapists had tried to teach him he learned much more effectively with the help of voluntary role playing with his plushies (stuffed animal friends). ABA only caused him trauma.

Most public schools in the US also use PBIS (positive behavioral interventions and supports), which is another form of ABA that leverages rewards in the form of tokens, points, and prizes to induce desirable behavior. PDA children almost always see through these tactics, and can react in a traumatized fashion, especially if their struggles at school mean they are excluded from rewards their peers are able to access.

Mainstream parenting strategies also rely on leveraging good and bad consequences to achieve desirable behavior. When done without applying awareness of the child's capacity for stressors or their unique triggers, it forces children to compartmentalize their stress or blow up.

Forcing neurodivergent children, or adults, to mask sets them up for a lifetime of ceding their needs, mental health, and identity to others. We believe this is one of the reasons why neurodivergent people are prone to being in abusive relationships (see Chapter 9).

We explore alternative, non-harmful therapies for PDA kids, and adults, in Chapter 10.

> **Brook:** Work settings were very hard for me because everyone there was supposed to be driven. There was no space for me to talk about how exhausted I was by normal work activities without looking "lazy," so I had to hide this side of myself, which made me feel more exhausted and alienated.

Indirectly imposed masking

The situation can be even worse for members of racially marginalized communities who have no access to people they can use as "blueprints" for building effective masks. Distress increases if failing to mask differences makes these community members targets for bullies. For example, it's impossible to mask skin tone from racist people. Responding to pressure to "act more white" can cause non-white people to uphold white supremacy at the expense of their entire community. Anika Campbell, a Black PDA adult, helped us by reading through our book and contributing to this section.

Masking can be imposed indirectly if a person is disadvantaged or feels vulnerable to attack because they don't match the societal norm. In this sense, it can be thought of as a survival strategy.

The imbalance is even more pronounced for members of our community who are marginalized due to race or ethnicity. The Black community uses the term "code switching" to describe the need to adopt different language and mannerisms to avoid standing out within white power structures because they are unable to "mask" their skin color. In this context, masking is a survival strategy for countering ingrained racial prejudice.

It's important to remember that each racial minority has its own experience of racism, including, but not limited to:

- history of oppression from white-dominated culture
- having to navigate systems built on demeaning stereotypes
- being part of intersecting vulnerable subcultures (e.g., being femme presenting)
- blindness to racial oppression from these intersecting subcultures
- members of their race staying silent, or even upholding oppressive systems.

This makes it harder for members of racially marginalized communities who have limited access to peers they can follow as "blueprints" for building these complex, overlapping masks.

Masking as adaptive communication

Adaptive communication refers to actively changing how we speak, what body language we use, and even what we wear to enhance the effectiveness of our social intercourse. We are using the term "adaptive communication" to describe a voluntary choice an individual makes to compensate for gaps in their ability to use body language, and other aspects of communication, in order to put others at ease without violating their own or anyone else's essential needs and boundaries.

Adaptive communication differs from the indirectly forced masking that vulnerable minorities use for self-preservation because it's a "peacetime" strategy for navigating relatively safe social situations. For instance, it enables us to be accepted into peer groups that we like the idea of being part of, but with no toll of danger if we fail to blend in. In this sense, adaptive communication differs from imposed masking because it is carried out for pleasure, and it isn't painful, even if it requires emotional resources to utilize. It's comparable to learning a foreign language as a hobby.

However, if someone is burnt out or overwhelmingly stressed, they are unlikely to be able to employ adaptive communication, let alone enjoy it, because they have too little emotional capacity for relaxed social interplay.

A key component of adaptive communication is social mimicry, which means copying tones of voice, postures, and mannerisms. Studies suggest that social mimicry is an unconscious human instinct which increases in intensity the more a person believes themself to be different from the social norm.[2] Perhaps unsurprisingly, many neurodivergent people say they socially mimic.

Adaptive communication can manifest as being charming. We saw in Chapter 1 that PDA people often employ charm to increase the effectiveness of their social interactions. The results of a 2018 peer study by Sally Cat[3] support the idea that social mimicry is carried out by neurotypical people as well as autistics.

Examples of adaptive communication are speaking and dressing formally when in formal company, and exaggerating a local accent to match the way another person talks. The motivation is to improve communication by putting the other party at ease and making it easier for them to grasp what we're saying. This benefits us too because it makes the other person more likely to respond in the way that we want. This might be as simple as to have them accept us into their group (e.g., if watching a sports match in a bar), or it could involve a more material benefit, such as being successful in a job interview.

As for social mimicry, we see adaptive communication as an instinctive social strategy that's used by all people, bar some autistic people. After all, autism cannot be diagnosed unless a social communication difference is present. We posit that one of these qualifying differences is having no instinctive drive to adapt our communication. This would explain why autistic people face so much societal pressure to mask.

There appears to be a parallel between adaptive communication and the instinctive submissive behavior that strong animals use to preempt conflict by appearing non-threatening, friendly, and playful (think of a dog rolling on its back and wagging its tail). In comparison, imposed masking can be thought of as using a whip to train a lion to jump through hoops, or by engaging in passive-aggressive ploys to deny safe, emotional connection to a person who's not "performing" in a way that's considered acceptable.

Sally: There were builders hanging around my rented home for a day or two. They were loud and spoke with a strong local accent. I was aware of trying to mirror their jokey communication style and replicate their dialect. I was delighted when my attempts at joining their banter succeeded. I loved feeling accepted into their closed peer group.

This type of role playing paid dividends when I was studying art in further education. I bought a "how to" book for the course and happily role played the geeky perfect student the book described. My tutor excitedly told me that I was the first ever student to receive a score of 100% from the external examiner.

Pain-masking behavior

The term "pain-masking behavior" was first used to describe prey animals' instinct to hide signs of injury and pain in order to avoid being targeted by predators.[4] Although no formal studies have been carried out, many PDA kids, and adults, seem to instinctively hide their pain and vulnerability too. An example is a child having a painful accident, but remaining perfectly still and showing no hint of distress in their facial expression.

We believe that because the nature of pain-masking behavior is to instinctively contain pain and distress within a calm facade, it's the driver behind internalized PDA and, as we'll see, spare play and situational mutism.

Sally: My daughter denied being in pain from the moment she'd mastered enough communication ability to do so. We'd never disapproved of her crying or showing distress, but she always panicked if we witnessed her being in pain, and would insist that she was OK.

Our parental instinct was to hug her, but this caused her to panic more. We learned that the only way to comfort her after she'd been hurt was to hold our arms open, without making direct eye contact, so she could choose to come to one of us for a cuddle, and that we mustn't make a big deal about her cuddling us either.

Spare play

Another hidden sign of PDA, and autism in general, is "tandem" or "spare play," whereby a child skips about the schoolyard so it looks as if they're playing with others, but close observation reveals that they're not interacting with anyone else at all.

The term "spare games" was coined by a nine-year-old client of British speech and language consultant Libby Hill, who says she's since met many other PDA and general autistic children who also do this.[5] Some of Libby's young, spare-gaming clients told her they preferred playing alone, but others said they wished they could play with their classmates. Both Sally Cat and her daughter have spare played. However, while Sally, as a child, hated feeling like a social failure and was depressed and ashamed to be shunned in the school playground, her daughter complained that her classmates pestered her to play, and said she preferred playing alone.

Even if a child wishes to play solo, spare playing is used to mask social isolation. If we remember that "pain-masking" behavior is an evolutionary strategy to conceal weakness from predators, spare playing serves that purpose. After all, lone prey animals are easier to pick off than ones in the middle of a herd. Of course, spare-playing children aren't protecting themselves from the eyes of prowling lions, but the instinct doesn't differentiate.

An important consideration with spare play is that many teachers, school administrators, and visiting assessors don't know to look out for it, and can assume the child in question has no social difficulties because they appear to be playing with their peers. The trick is to keep on watching the child. If they're spare playing, it soon becomes clear that they're not interacting with their peers at all.

Sally: As a child, I had energy to play, but no one to play with me because I couldn't connect with my peers. I'd switch into my latest immersive daydream scenario. A favorite fantasy

> involved me living in a wooden hut in a forest with tame fawns, and skipping around acting it out.

Situational mutism

Situational mutism, sometimes termed "selective mutism," means being completely quiet and unmoving during certain social situations, such as in school, but not in others. It's characterized by having a frozen, rigid facial expression. It's caused by extreme anxiety and sets in after toddlerhood. It tends to show up after children are compelled to interact with people outside their close family circle—for example, when they start going to preschool. It seems to be very common for PDA kids, and is also experienced by some PDA adults. Situational muteness varies in intensity. A child might be able to talk in front of their class, but not one on one to individual classmates.

Libby Hill advises letting situationally mute children develop at their own pace and in their own way, without pressuring them to talk more.

> **Brook:** Before any of us knew much about autism, or anything about PDA, my oldest showed indicators that something different was going on with him than with his peers. He would freely talk verbally with both of his parents and his siblings, but around anyone else he either pantomimed what he needed or he whispered it (albeit loudly) in my ear.
>
> Because he otherwise seemed engaged socially (joking with his gestures, responding to my jokes by smiling), when we tried to get him diagnosed, his autism was dismissed. I was blamed for his mutism even though the examples of how I was "enabling" it didn't fit with how I treated my child. I was blamed.

CHAPTER 3

Adrenal Defense Strategies

The purpose of this chapter is to shine light onto why PDA children, and adults, may behave in reckless and/or antisocial ways, and show how dysfunctional dynamics within family relationships can be soothed. Once triggers are understood, peaceful bridges can be built.

A popular way of categorizing trauma reactions is called "The F trauma/adrenal responses." The primary responses identified are fight, flight, and freeze, but in more recent history fawn and flop have also been included. Another recently proposed F response is fibbing.

We believe the range of Fs is actually even greater and have penned names for three additional adrenal responses: fantasy, funster, and forget. Our go-to F responses may be situational. For example, someone who defaults to fight with their family may fawn with people they know less well. It may seem to observers that a PDA child's adrenal reactions are baseless, or contrived to attract attention, but the underlying reality is that their behavior is driven by blind panic.

It should be borne in mind that our adrenal reactions are inherited from the animal kingdom. We, as a species, would have been wiped out eons ago, having fallen prey to marauding leopards and all the other dangers our adrenal defense strategies have evolved to protect us from.

Brook: When I wanted to learn more about PDA, I read story after story to try to understand how it worked for others through human eyes. What struck me was how, on a surface level, families had different struggles. One family had a child who was compliant in school; another child melted down in front of strangers. Some children silently retreated into a fantasy world, and their parents were terrified of losing them completely. Another child ran around, relentlessly teasing siblings and friends. It fascinated me that the same driver could be behind such a wide range of external appearances.

At the same time, I'd been learning about complex trauma because of personal family complexities that led to my divorce and three rattled kids. There was very little judgment in trauma support groups about the violent, explosive behaviors my fellow members were capable of.

Commonalities were often noted between groups of people whose behavior could be tied to identifiable trauma and to those who, like PDA people, seemed born ready to react to the world traumatically.

OVERVIEW OF INDIVIDUAL Fs

To our minds, it's important to understand all the ways in which people can respond to threats in order to understand PDA, because our naturally high anxiety causes our adrenal glands to continually pump stress hormones through our systems to trigger these responses.

Fight

Fight is, perhaps, the easiest F response to grasp, because triggered adrenaline causes visible aggression. Often, this is considered a "meltdown" in the context of autistic behavior. The fight mode is brought on by adrenaline coursing through the body, which causes the heart rate to increase and muscles to tense, so the person is primed and ready to tackle incoming threats head-on.

Traditional descriptions of PDA describe children whose default adrenal response is fight. In fact, the first scale to measure PDA—the EDA-Q—down-scored children who don't default to the fight response. For example, #13: "If pressurised to do something, s/he may have a 'meltdown' (e.g. scream, tantrum, hit or kick)."[1] Although the fight-primed version of PDA is the one that's been written about, we don't believe it to be PDA's primary form. Our belief is that the fighty version of our condition has been written about because it's the easiest presentation to spot. In fact, logically speaking, PDA people should, surely, be more likely to default to the flight response because fleeing is the most direct way to avoid things.

> **Brook:** "Fighting" feels very vulnerable to me, so I usually only express this reaction to my safe people. If I am in public, it used to take a lot for me to feel like it was safe to show this expression. One time during a Bible Study, I lashed out at friends because they observed me crying (another very vulnerable expression for me) and I felt so overwhelmed by their concern that I snapped at them, angrily, to get away.

Flight

Flight, like fight, tends to be obvious to observers because, in the case of flight, the individual simply runs away. As in fight, flight mode is activated by adrenaline, which causes the heart rate to increase. However, unlike in fight, the person is desperate to escape the threatening situation and can experience a panic attack.

> **Sally:** I'm much more prone to flight than fight. I have a tendency to dash blindly out of busy shopping centers and discharge myself early from hospital stays. Employment has been particularly difficult for me because of my overriding need to flee confinement.

Freeze

The next best-known F response is freeze, which differs from fight and flight because the heart rate decreases. The freeze state is an inability to move brought about by the adrenal gland releasing cortisol as well as adrenaline so that fight and flight are put on hold. As a result, the person, or animal, has time to assess the threat and how best to deal with it. A classic example of freeze is a rabbit being caught motionless in a car's headlights.

> **Sally:** My personal experiences of the freeze response have been traumatic, with me feeling horrendously anxious, but totally unable to physically protect myself, either by fighting or running away.

Fawn

Fawning means avoiding conflict by people-pleasing—putting our own needs last and hiding our true feelings, even though doing this often compromises our own well-being. "Fawning" is often used synonymously with "masking" because it involves people acting as if nothing's wrong with them when they feel threatened.

The fawn response is associated with complex post-traumatic stress disorder (CPTSD), which develops after people have been subjected to long-term trauma, such as domestic violence and emotional or sexual abuse. The term "fawn" was coined by a complex trauma specialist, named Pete Walker, who identified it as a survival strategy children developed after prolonged parental abuse, from which fight, flight, and freeze had been unable to defend them.[2] We speculate that fawning is a dysregulated expression of adaptive communication (see "Masking as adaptive communication" in Chapter 2).

As two of PDA's core traits are proneness to anxiety and social focus, it's maybe not surprising that many PDA adults say fawning is their default adrenal response, often adding that they hate it. We question the belief that fawning is always a submissive behavior, because panicked people-pleasing can be used to establish power over others, especially when driven by a control-needing PDA brain.

> **Brook:** When I fawn, it comes across as dominating. I try to use my skills to "help" people by teaching them, or advocating for them, but I have learned that this instinct can get out of hand when I'm doing it from a place of fear. If I'm not careful, I get into imbalanced dynamics where I'm the helper, and the other person is the submitter.

Flop

Flop, like fawn, has gained recognition as an additional adrenal reaction to supplement the classic fight, flight, freeze threesome. While flopping may appear to be a soft adrenal reaction, there is nothing soft about its root cause. A UK rape charity says that flop is similar to freezing, "except your muscles become loose and your body goes floppy. This is an automatic reaction that can reduce the physical pain of what's happening to you. Your mind can also shut down to protect itself."[3]

An easy-to-grasp example of flop is fainting: in other words physically, and mentally, flopping onto the ground like a collapsed rag doll. Another example of flopping is falling asleep when faced with a high-pressure situation.

> **Brook:** When my kids come to me unexpectedly, and ask me to play games with them, I immediately feel drowsy.

Fib

Fibbing, or telling lies, is a socio-linguistic defense strategy used when the threat comes from another person, or group of people, who will harm the individual because of something they said or did. Fib mode kicks in if the fight/flight reaction commanded by surging adrenal hormones is, first, diverted into freezing, then, second, the threat is interpreted as negative judgment against us, which could be best tackled by using social and linguistic skills to deny culpability.

According to an article in the online ADHD magazine *ADDitude Mag*, "With complex and advanced language (not available to our primitive ancestors), we have the ability to verbalize both factual and/or fictitious reasoning instantaneously at point of performance, most notably in times of stress and threat."[4]

Parents of PDA kids frequently talk of their children lying about things they've been caught doing. Fibbing is referenced in the EDA-Q, which, as we've seen, was the first scale for measuring PDA. Question 18 is: "Denies behavior s/he has committed, even when caught red handed?"[5] As most autistic kids and adults find it difficult to lie, fibbing is another trait that sets PDA apart from general autism.[6]

> **Sally:** When my daughter fibs, I'm conscious that she's incredibly anxious about something she's hiding, and that direct confrontation would merely terrify her more. She'll already be learning lessons about not repeating whatever it is she's felt driven to hide. I feel it is better to comfort her and let her know in a general, un-heavy way, that she's supported and loved.

Funster

Funster, like fib, is a socially adapted F adrenal defense strategy. It involves playing the clown to simultaneously hide our own vulnerable true-selves and de-escalate hostility towards us.

When in funster mode, people play the clown and fool about

in an attention-grabbing manner. There will likely be a sense that the funster is panicked behind their smiling facade. The term "funster" was coined by Sally Cat, in 2021,[7] after she realized that the mischievous outbursts both she and her daughter had carried out were anxiety-driven, and that this type of behavior was frequently described by other members of the PDA community. As we've seen from *ADDitude* magazine's article, quoted in the "Fib" section, above, it's believed that complex, social adrenal reactions have evolved alongside our linguistic ability.

> **Sally:** I can clearly relate to having gone into funster mode when I felt intense social anxiety. The fun, joking, clown persona that resulted wasn't something I felt in control of. For example, when on holiday with my best friend and her boyfriend (who I didn't feel relaxed or confident with), I spent the duration of our shared time in full-on funster mode. Consciously, I just wanted to make them laugh. Internally, I was in a constant state of panic.

Fantasy

As we saw in Chapter 1, being drawn to fantasy and/or role play is considered a core trait of PDA. Fantasy serves an important purpose for the human psyche by helping us imagine possibilities, but when triggered as a trauma response, fantasizing reaches into extremes that can harm us and our relationships. For some, this looks like maladaptive daydreaming where the dreamer escapes into their inner world, for large portions of time, in order to cope.

Fantasy can also be used to create artificial worlds of explanations, which prevent the fantasist from confronting their fears. This can manifest as deflecting blame from ourselves onto others, which is listed as a qualifying trait in the EDA-Q.[8]

Scapegoating can be considered an expression of the fantasy adrenal response because it's a defense mechanism by which the scapegoater blames their target for fantasized crimes. A large number of PDA adults, Sally Cat included, have said that their own mother, or some other close family member, scapegoated them. See also the sections on mirrored personality disorders in Chapter 8 and protective narcissism in Chapter 9.

PDA is believed to be a genetic condition. From observation, it appears to affect whole generations without any family member realizing that their strong, changeable emotions, anxiety, drive to avoid, and other difficulties are caused by their inherited neurology. It's perhaps unsurprising that some parents of PDA kids, who don't realize that they are PDA themselves, make sense of the high pressures churning inside them by assigning blame to their children. Child blaming is, alas, so common in online PDA parenting groups that PDA parents aware of this risk, like Brook Madera, run alternative groups in which child blaming is closely monitored.

> **Brook:** My use of fantasy is creating backstories to account for why certain stressful things are happening, so that I can talk myself into feeling safe. The problem is that if I don't check with the real world on occasion, I can talk myself into being safe in situations that aren't a fit for me, and only continue to traumatize me.

Forget

Forgetting, in the context of F adrenal strategies, is similar to flop and fantasy because it's an inactive response which, in the case of forget, deals with threats by forgetting about them (a bit like the proverbial ostrich burying its head in the sand).

The most well-known version of "forgetting" during trauma is dissociation, where the individual experiences a "detachment or feeling as if one is outside one's body, and a loss of memory or amnesia."[9] Forgetting can also happen as short-term bursts of forgetfulness when put on the spot to provide answers. Another example is using substances like alcohol and drugs that induce forgetfulness.

> **Brook:** As soon as I'm anxious, forgetting is the first thing that happens. I forget what I'm doing, I forget simple answers to questions. I have to intentionally address my anxiety and

> relax myself in order to access my memory, especially in social settings.

Flood

Flood is sometimes cited as an additional adrenal reaction, but it lacks a specific definition. Literature describes it as a PTSD "meltdown" involving fighting, fleeing, and crying. The tearful element of flood is interesting because crying is the first social "distress" communication we're equipped with as babies born into our complex, socially dynamic society.

As authors who are PDA ourselves, we admit to having used tears as leverage for manipulating outcomes in our favor. In this sense, crying, like fawning, may be thought of as a submissive-seeming defense strategy that can be wielded as a means of gaining control.

ADRENAL DEFENSES AND MASKING

In the last chapter, we proposed that there are four types of human masking, of which one is imposed and unhealthy, and two are inherited, preemptive defense strategies that evolved in the animal kingdom. We put the case that adaptive communication equates to strong animals' submissive behavior, by which conflict is preempted by communicating non-threatening friendliness. We also proposed that pain-masking behavior, by which prey animals hide their weakness from predators, explains internalized PDA in humans.

We theorize that when cortisol blends with adrenaline so that fight and flight are put on hold (freeze), time is given for our brains' instinctive masking to influence which defensive strategy is used when the body unfreezes. Adaptive communication and pain-masking behavior often occur together, so the individual carries them out simultaneously. Both masking types seem to influence how adrenal reactions are expressed. We believe that fawning behavior is more submissive when the pain-masking drive is strong, and more assertive when the drive to use adaptive communication dominates.

It seems probable that the masking type we use at any given

time accords with the nature of the person we feel threatened by. For example, if we're confronted with a bully, we might slip into pain-masking behavior so they can't find weaknesses to exploit. If, on the other hand, the person in question comes across as appraising, rather than bullying, and is in possession of something we want, we might use adaptive communication to attempt to win them over. An example of this could be using charm during a meeting with a potential landlord.

Adaptive communication and pain-masking behavior seem to feed into fibbing which, after all, is about adapting communication to evade having our fault observed. Funster, too, may be seen as a socially adaptive strategy for disarming perceived hostility by hiding our own anxiety and making people laugh.

POLYVAGAL THEORY

Polyvagal theory is often mentioned in conjunction with PDA and merits a mention in this chapter about adrenaline responses. We'd like to thank the renowned speech and language therapist Libby Hill for collaborating with us on this section, because she understands the theory very well.

Polyvagal theory, which was put forward by Stephen Porges in 1994,[10] is a model of a tiered nervous system. It can be thought of as a descending spectrum of nervous system states, linked by what's termed "the autonomic ladder." The upper nervous state is a feel-good one, while the lower ones make people feel ill at ease and sick to their guts.

The ventral vagal system is the one at the top of the autonomic ladder. It operates when all is well. It keeps the good feelings going by inhibiting adrenaline reactions through self-soothing and social engagement. If someone experiences sustained trauma, the ventral vagal nervous system shuts down, and the person's functioning descends the autonomic ladder to the sympathetic and dorsal nervous systems, which take over instead.

In brief, the sympathetic nervous system is a network of nerves that are primed for the fight/flight/freeze reaction, and the dorsal nervous system is a large, primitive part of the vagal nerves that controls body functions, such as digestion.

According to Libby, if we look at the work of Deb Dana,[11] who's worked a lot with Stephen Porges, when we're feeling good, we're operating at the top of the autonomic ladder. Our ventral vagal nerve is in control, so that we feel relaxed and move about the world with ease. At the same time, our sympathetic nervous system buzzes along, regulating our blood flow and heart rate, and our dorsal vagal system keeps our body digesting, resting when it needs to, and restoring itself. Everything's good, and this is how it's all supposed to work.

However, this happy, buzzing nervous symphony halts the moment our neuroception—our inbuilt threat detection system—detects anything amiss. Think of a dog who starts growling the moment that they hear a noise outside. If spooked, people automatically seek the faces or voices of others for reassurance, and this has an immediate calming effect on our nervous systems, so that we don't escalate into defense mode.

If our neuroception decides there is a threat, our ventral vagal system shuts down, and our sympathetic and dorsal nervous systems take over. When dominant, our sympathetic nervous system makes us feel uneasy, lose cognitive ability, disconnect socially, and mobilize for fight, flight, freeze, or, perhaps, one of the lesser-known F reactions. At the same time, our dorsal vagal system can make our guts start churning—as the saying goes, having butterflies in the stomach. If you've watched the TV series *Stranger Things*, descending the autonomic ladder is like entering the nightmare world of the Upside Down.

Sustained trauma can cause the sympathetic nervous system to shut down, as well as the ventral vagal system, leaving the dorsal system in complete control. When this happens, digestive and system responses dominate us. This can cause things like irritable bowel syndrome and mast cell activation syndrome (allergic reactions to stressors, such as hives).

If the dorsal system remains dominant for a long time, long-term issues can develop as a result of the body being in crisis for far too long, in a nervous system state it shouldn't be in. According to Libby, possible health impacts are food intolerances, Crohn's disease, fibromyalgia, ME/CFS, or long-term burnout.

How polyvagal theory connects to PDA

According to polyvagal theory, tolerance and control decrease as demands and anxiety increase. This can happen for anyone, but PDA people are naturally primed for it because needing personal control is a core trait of PDA.

When a PDA person perceives a demand, our inherent avoidance drive is triggered. In polyvagal terms, the perceived demand shuts down our ventral vagal system so that our sympathetic nervous system leaps into action, causing a feeling of intense unease, and mobilizing us for fight/flight/freeze/etc. adrenal responses.

Polyvagal theory, therefore, explains PDA people's proneness to adrenal responses by way of our demand avoidance continually triggering our sympathetic nervous system to take over. However, as we'll see in the next chapter, polyvagal theory doesn't account for the irrational, pathological nature of our avoidance.

CHAPTER 4

Other Conditions

It's important to distinguish PDA from similar-seeming conditions so that appropriate support can be implemented.

> **Sally:** I've come across a lot of people, including parents and clinicians, who see neurodivergent diagnoses as stigmas which ruin people's lives, be they young or old.
>
> For example, a teacher friend was angry when I told her about my dyslexia diagnosis because she thought I used it to avoid making an effort, lamenting that her dyslexic pupils did this. I explained that the reverse was true in my case, because my adult diagnosis of dyslexia had given me confidence to try harder. Pre-diagnosis, I'd assumed myself incapable of learning and had sat in a slump of not trying at all.

Every adult neurodivergent diagnosis I've gained has felt liberating and empowering. I think of them as Brownie badges. I've worked hard to gain each diagnosis, and every one has enhanced my self-esteem and ability to function in society. I spent my entire life chronically depressed until, piece by piece, my accumulation of neurodivergent diagnoses raised my self-esteem.

My diagnoses to date are PDA, autism, ADHD, delayed sleep phase syndrome, ME, dyslexia, and dyspraxia. I also believe I pass the diagnostic threshold for many of the other conditions, including Tourette's syndrome and dyscalculia, but haven't accessed assessment for these so far.

CO-OCCURRING CONDITIONS

It wasn't so long ago that autism and ADHD were deemed so unlikely to co-occur that ADHD diagnoses couldn't be given if autism had already been diagnosed. The reality, however, seems to be that autism, ADHD, and other conditions, such as Tourette's and dyslexia, seem more likely to cluster than crop up solo. Added to this mix are physical conditions, like Ehlers–Danlos syndromes and fibromyalgia. The likelihood of these conditions clustering is borne out by a poll Sally Cat carried out in 2021. Participants in this informal peer research had six co-occurring conditions on average, but only 3.7 percent of respondents reported having one condition only.[1]

ADHD

PDA and ADHD occurring together generate avoidance on many levels. ADHD causes tasks to be forgotten or, if remembered, painful to focus on. PDA avoidance can involve being ultra-aware of tasks our brain has commanded us to avoid. When ADHD and PDA co-occur, things can get messy because we're aware of some things we're avoiding, while unaware of others.

Windows of opportunity can be precariously brief, necessitating that we act before the ADHD part of our brain forgets and the PDA part of us slams down its virtual portcullis of demand avoidance. A real-life example of dealing with this, reported by many PDA-ADHD folk (us included), is to respond to emails immediately before our brains make doing so impossible via a combination of demand avoidance and forgetfulness.

ADHD hyperfocus and PDA avoidance can pull us in different directions. Hyperfocus can be strong enough to override demand avoidance so that a project can be engaged with, but demand avoidance can then keep niggling that individual details—such as painting a whole area, or researching something in depth—should be avoided.

However, not all PDA people identify as also being ADHD. This is backed up by a peer study Sally Cat ran, in which, of 224 respondents identifying as PDA, 29 percent said: "I don't have ADD [attention deficit disorder] or ADHD and have not had issues with being hyper or inattentive."[2] It should also be borne in mind that there are people who are both autistic and ADHD but are not actually PDA (see AuDHD later in this chapter).

Complicating things further, PDA masking can hide signs of ADHD so well that assessors fail to spot it.

> **Sally:** My daughter masked her hyperactivity so well in school that only one professional (an educational psychologist) noticed that, though rigidly motionless, her eyes were constantly looking around the room. For me, I'm aware of pressing my fingertips tightly together instead of outwardly expressing my need for physical movement.

Autism

As things stand, PDA can only be diagnosed as a behavioral description within a diagnosis of autism spectrum disorder. This is met with a variety of reactions from mild skepticism to outright denial. Some of this is due to limited stereotypes around the range of what autism looks like, but we also believe some conflict is due to legitimate and distinct differences between PDA and non-PDA autism.

For autism to be diagnosed, there must be social communication difficulties and rigid thinking. People who categorize PDA as autism class demand avoidance and/or having social fixations as rigid thinking. Instead of obsessing about trains, a PDA person might fixate on people and relationships. To give a different example, in place of sticking to routines, as many autistic people do,[3] PDA people's unshakeable demand avoidance can be argued to qualify as autistic rigid thinking.[4] With regard to social communication difficulties, a PDA person may mask social blind spots. Skeptics may argue that because PDA and non-PDA autistic people need dramatically different support strategies, grouping the two together generates confusion and hinders the spread of PDA awareness.

Some autistic people object to naming separate autism profiles, such as Asperger's syndrome, arguing that the practice is outdated and divisive. Through that lens, PDA is part of the "unfenced field" of potential autism traits. This view of PDA is fueled by the condition being named for demand avoidance only, giving the impression that it is a form of extreme demand avoidance that any autistic person may experience. However, in reality, PDA is hallmarked by a cluster of other traits (such as high control need and social focus), and our "pathological" brand of demand avoidance is unique to PDA.

Others believe PDA is a condition in its own right, in the same way that ADHD frequently co-occurs with autism, but doesn't always. The fact that PDA people need different support from that which is effective for general autism does suggest that it may be a distinct condition.

> **Brook:** My autism takes comfort in the familiar patterns in methods that I use for things. I am constantly juggling my need for comfort in routine with my need for novelty and freedom that go along with my ADHD and PDA. Also trying to learn from my social interactions and how to apply that knowledge in my daily relationships has taken me decades to work out.

Nonspeaking autism

It's estimated that between 25 and 35 percent of autistic people are nonspeaking.[5] This means never speaking or having spoken language that's limited on all occasions.[6] Although some professionals term this group "nonverbal," the community itself prefers to call themselves "nonspeaking."[7] Families who suspect their nonspeaking children are also PDA report challenges with them using the recommended augmented and alternative communication (AAC) devices, which nonspeaking autistics rely on, because using the device is perceived as a demand. Aside from troubleshooting any practical obstacles to using an AAC device, success for supporting PDA can lie in having all family members using the same device to communicate (making all parties equal) and offering choices in what kind of AAC the PDA child may use (providing a level of personal control to reduce the perception of demand).

Avoidant/restrictive food intake disorder (ARFID)

The term ARFID was introduced by the DSM-5 in 2013.[8] ARFID was previously called selective eating disorder. It involves avoiding certain foods or food groups and/or eating only small amounts. This behavior isn't related to food availability, cultural practices, fasting for religious reasons, or wanting to lose weight.

While the exact causes are unclear, ARFID may stem from sensory sensitivities, fear of negative experiences with food (e.g., choking or vomiting), or a lack of interest in eating. ARFID can affect individuals of any age, even children as young as two.[9] Research suggests that it's more common for autistic people than for the rest of the population.[10]

PDA kids, and adults, may be especially prone to ARFID because of the irrational nature of our demand avoidance that can tell us to avoid pleasurable things we need, such as eating when hungry (see the section "'Pathological' demand avoidance" in Chapter 1). Pressure around eating—like finishing our meals and eating enough vegetables—can also trigger our avoidance. The more a parent or carer pressures us to eat something, no matter how benignly, the more our avoidance of eating it may heighten.

The recommendation for dealing with ARFID is to support the kid's food refusal, rather than trying to force them to eat stuff, or tricking them into eating hidden things like vegetables.[11] ARFID can continue through childhood and beyond, and can be hard to support because the demands of nutrition and any medical intervention are likely to add to the stress load.

> **Sally:** I had massive struggles with food as a child. I avoided some foods because of hypersensitivity. For example, cabbages tasted overwhelmingly bitter, and the texture of boiled fruit reminded me of snot. I avoided other foods because they felt forced on me (like when my mum went to the trouble to cook my brother's favorite dish). Sometimes I was terrified that foods—such as lettuce that a bug had touched—would contaminate me. On other occasions, I vetoed food because I was spooked after hallucinating random things, like Mahjong game pieces in my bowl of porridge.

Circadian sleep disorders (CSDs)

These are conditions caused by the body's central regulating clock running at a rate that's stubbornly out of sync with the social norm. Advanced sleep-wake phase disorder (ASWD) is a circadian (body clock) sleep disorder that causes people's sleep-wake cycles to be far earlier than the social norm. ASWD people struggle to stay awake for evening functions and wake during the small hours of the morning.

Delayed sleep phase syndrome (DSPS), sometimes referred to as delayed sleep phase disorder, is a circadian clock disorder that causes people's sleep-wake schedules to be markedly later than the social norm—for example, having a natural sleep cycle of 4 a.m. through to midday. It can be thought of as jetlag that never resets.

Non-24 sleep-wake disorder (Non-24) is a circadian sleep disorder which, like DSPS, is caused by the body's clock running slowly but, in the case of Non-24, the circadian clock dominates so the person's sleep-wake times run forward, later and later every day/night, until they cycle right through the entire 24 hour clock in an endless, progressive loop.

DSPS and Non-24 can be particularly debilitating in our morning-biased society. Inflexible schedules, such as 7 a.m. school start times, can, and do, cause major sleep deprivation. This can exacerbate a PDA child's drive to avoid school.

More detailed information is provided on the Circadian Sleep Disorders Network's website.[12] Additionally, Sally Cat's book Sleep Misfits is available via Amazon worldwide.[13]

> **Sally:** My sleep-wake cycle has been severely delayed since my early childhood. This made getting up in time for school very painful because I used to be so sleep-deprived. I felt ashamed about my late sleeping and waking until I discovered that DSPS is known to science and has nothing to do with me being lazy or weak-willed.
>
> Though I'm used to the world being morning-biased, my PDA social equalizing drive* triggers anger alongside my demand avoidance if I'm expected to lose sleep because of an inflexible, early deadline—for example, having to checkout of accommodation before 9 a.m.
>
> * See Chapter 5.

Ehlers–Danlos syndromes (EDS) and hypermobility

EDS is frequently mentioned by members of the PDA community, both by parents/carers and by adults for whom EDS co-occurs with their PDA. EDS is an umbrella term which encompasses a range of disorders affecting the connective tissues that support skin, bones, blood vessels, and other organs.[14] A classic symptom of EDS is hypermobility, which means people can bend their joints in ways others can't. It makes people prone to joint pains, sprains, and even dislocation. There are different types of EDS, which have different impacts on health and require professionals to help manage them.

EDS may add an extra layer of complexity for PDA folk grappling with their brain's resistance to physical demands, such as personal hygiene or participating in sport at school.

> **Brook:** My son's hypermobility is fairly mild, but he has often complained about pain if we try to go on long walks, which adds to the demand load of activities. I now bring a covered wagon if we go anywhere and it serves as a safe way for him to retreat when he gets overwhelmed by pain, overstimulation, and any combination of demands that come with leaving the home.

Fibromyalgia and ME/chronic fatigue syndrome

Fibromyalgia and ME are central sensitivity syndromes which involve chronic fatigue, pain, and brain fog (cognitive impairment). Fibromyalgia involves more pain than ME.[15] Even without the pain, these conditions can be hugely disabling, making it impossible to do more than a tiny number of tasks per day. As a core trait of PDA is avoiding life's everyday tasks, co-occurring fibromyalgia or ME make it even harder to get anything done. Picture the scenario: you finally overcome a wall of demand avoidance against tidying your bedroom and start picking up dirty clothes when you suddenly feel dizzy and your energy cuts out like someone's flicked off a light. People watching might think we made no effort at all.

> **Sally:** I developed chronic fatigue when my daughter was a baby. Of all my many invisible conditions, I'd say that my ME, PDA, and delayed sleep phase syndrome impact me the most. I have to limit how much energy I use so that I don't crash (the PDA part of my brain loves this because it gives me an excuse to avoid doing most things!).

Hyperlexia

The term "hyperlexia" is used for children whose reading ability is way above what's expected for their age. Hyperlexic adults have greater reading ability than their peers. When hyperlexia overlaps with PDA, it impacts the level of demand associated with different forms of communication. For example, written information is less likely to trigger demand avoidance than it might for non-hyperlexic PDA folk.[16]

> **Brook:** I find myself far more comfortable with reading the written word than hearing it spoken, and can move faster through it, even use it as a comfort when I'm stressed and anxious. When I try to listen to the same information, I feel like I have to gather more energy to focus.

Learning disabilities[17]

We consider it important to differentiate between intellectual disabilities that affect overall cognitive ability and "dyssy" conditions, such as dyslexia and dyspraxia, which don't affect general intelligence and only impact specific things, such as learning to read.[18]

Cognitive impairment, sometimes called intellectual disability, refers to people with IQ scores below 70.[19] People often think that this type of learning disability is part of autism, and that its existence makes a person's autism more "profound" or "severe."[20] The reality is that these are separate conditions that frequently co-occur.[21]

"Dyssy" conditions are termed "learning difficulties" in the UK because they make learning certain things challenging, but not impossible. They include dyslexia (specifically associated with reading and writing), dyscalculia (mathematics and numbers), dyspraxia (physical coordination), and dysgraphia (difficulty with handwriting).

When co-occurring with PDA, all forms of learning difficulty are likely to compound demand avoidance. For example, while the inherent demands of the education system tend to challenge most PDA kids, dyslexia ramps up the stress attached to mandatory reading expectations.

> **Brook:** My son is a great artist, but he holds his pencil differently and it makes it harder for him to write his letters precisely. Instead, he compensates by making them larger and more elaborate.

> **Sally:** I'm blessed with a full house of "dyssy" conditions. My first neurodivergent diagnosis was dyslexia when I was at university, aged 30. I then heard about dyspraxia and gained a diagnosis for this too. Both diagnoses empowered me. I think this was because my PDA brain makes me avoid trying things by telling me I'm guaranteed to fail. But now I knew why I'd struggled with reading, spelling, and physical coordination and that failure wasn't the foregone conclusion that my demand-avoidant brain had convinced me of.

Mast cell activation syndrome (MCAS)

MCAS causes us to be abnormally prone to allergic reactions, such as hives, constricted airways, and irritable bowel syndrome. It's caused by having too many active mast cells, whose function is to protect our bodies from toxins by triggering allergic reactions.[22] Although little is known about MCAS, it has been mentioned frequently in PDA and other neurodivergent forums. Pertinently, it's thought that MCAS can be triggered by stress,[23] which PDA people are especially prone to. As we saw in the last chapter, polyvagal theory predicts that sustained stress causes physical reactions in the gut. Being physically sick from anxiety is, sadly, a common theme in PDA groups. When it occurs with PDA, MCAS is maybe similar to a canary in a coalmine, giving advance warning of anxiety outbreaks.

> **Sally:** I've had antihistamines prescribed for over ten years because I get hives when I'm sleep-deprived. Also, my body responds to anxiety by turning my guts to liquid and con-

> stricting my airways, so I have coughing fits. These physical symptoms let me know I'm anxious before I'm consciously aware of it.

Obsessive-compulsive disorder (OCD)

OCD involves unwanted, distressing thoughts (obsessions) that lead to repetitive actions (compulsions). These compulsions are performed to relieve anxiety caused by the obsessions, creating a cycle that's hard to break. OCD often revolves around specific fears, like contamination, which can lead to behaviors like excessive hand-washing.[24]

If a person is both OCD and PDA, the two conditions may clash. For example, a compulsion to backtrack home in case the faucets have been left running may trigger PDA avoidance against "having to" waste time and energy. Conversely, PDA avoidance against cleaning the kitchen might induce an OCD panic attack. In both examples, anxiety is escalated.

> **Brook:** One of my boys relies on ritual reassurances that increase the more anxious he gets. His desire for needing scripts backfires with our other PDA family members (myself included!) who are triggered by his demands, which can then spiral us all into anxious panic attacks.

Rejection sensitive dysphoria (RSD)

RSD is an extreme sensitivity to perceived rejection by other people. It can totally overwhelm us so that we can't think about anything else. People typically describe RSD as a deep emotional pain triggered by rejection, which can be difficult to describe because it's often much more intense than other types of emotional or physical pain.[25]

Although RSD is not a formal diagnosis, many clinicians recognize it. It's traditionally associated with ADHD, but other neurodivergent people report experiencing it. Although it may seem like a trauma response, it is believed to be caused by structural differences in the brain.[26] We have a hunch that, in some cases, RSD may result from high PDA anxiety clashing with social focus.

> **Brook:** I have done a lot of self work and have lessened how triggered I am by certain types of rejection that I can predict. Even so, my immediate instinct when something unexpectedly goes wrong is to try to think through all the ways I messed up. The stress from the automatic feeling of rejection can take me a week or more to process.

Sensory processing disorder (SPD)

Sensory processing disorder (SPD) impacts how the brain perceives incoming stimuli, such as taste, touch, sight, smells, and sound. It can be "hyper" (ramped up high) or "hypo" (pulled down low)—for example, experiencing background noise as unbearable (hyper) or finding it intolerable if there isn't background noise (hypo). It often co-occurs with autism, but it affects non-autistic people too.[27] When sensory processing disorder co-occurs with PDA in a "hyper" way, amplified sounds, tastes, textures, and other perceptions can bombard our brains with attention demands. Conversely, "hypo" sensory feedback can trigger our PDA brains to panic that the stimulation we need is being denied.

> **Brook:** My family experiences a few forms of sensory processing issues. Sometimes when I'm nervous, I feel the sudden urge to urinate even if my bladder is empty. I struggle too with processing auditory words if I'm not mentally prepared to receive them. Most of my learning I access through written words because it is easier for me to absorb.

Synesthesia

Synesthesia is a neurological condition that causes sensory inputs, or thoughts, to be experienced via unrelated senses. There are 60 or more forms of synesthesia. These include seeing letters as colors, hearing motion, and tasting shapes.[28]

Because both synesthesia and individual demand perception varies, there's no single way in which it interacts with PDA. For example, a synesthesiac PDA person who sees aromas might be triggered by the "shape" of a new food's smell. Alternatively, if a PDA person attaches specific colors to letters, they may struggle if somebody assigns a different color to the letter B.

> **Sally:** I'm lucky to have calendar synesthesia which stores my memories, dating back to babyhood, in a virtual reel that I can easily view like 3D video clips with tastes and smells attached.

Tourette's syndrome

Tourette's is a nervous system condition that causes involuntary twitches, movements, or sounds that are known as tics. Complex vocal tics include repeating phrases; complex physical tics include reaching to touch something.[29] Tourette's syndrome is thought to be more common than is often believed.[30] As for internalized PDA, tics can be diverted, so they're harder to spot.

> **Sally:** I'm pretty sure Tourette's is one of my many neurodivergent "Brownie badges." I have repeated impulses to blurt things out before my conscious brain has a chance to censor them. It's embarrassing. The split second that I realize I've started blurting something random, I mask it as best I can on the fly—for example, by switching into a comic voice to make it seem like I said the thing on purpose.

THINGS PDA IS MISTAKEN FOR

Attachment disorder (reactive)

High sociability with poor awareness of boundaries

Although both conditions involve people focus, social difficulties, and disregard of social boundaries, PDA also includes irrational demand avoidance and other distinct traits (see Chapter 1). Sadly, PDA being misidentified as reactive attachment disorder is a frequent topic in parent and carer support groups. The tragedy is that when professionals mistake PDA for attachment disorder, not only is appropriate support denied, but the parent or carer is blamed for their child's emotional dysregulation. Parent blame is examined in more detail in the discussion of fabricated or induced illness later in this section.

> **Robin Joyce:** My son was diagnosed with reactive attachment disorder at six years old. It devastated me as I had tried to be such a good mum (but not TOO intense as to make him anxious). I had no idea how I could have given him an attachment disorder. It just devastated me for months and made me hesitant to continue seeking professional support for him (but we were in such crisis, we had to). It took two more years and four more professionals to finally get an autism diagnosis, with a PDA profile.

Autism and ADHD combined (AuDHD)

Avoiding everyday tasks, being autistic, but liking novelty

The term "AuDHD" has recently become popular. People who have discovered that they are both autistic and ADHD embrace the term as a concise way to describe their neurological makeup. However, the concept of AuDHD may give the impression that neurodiversity comprises only autism, ADHD, and being neurotypical. This may cause other neurodivergent conditions, including PDA, to be overlooked. In this light, it shouldn't be surprising that some people assume AuDHD and PDA are the same thing.

The belief that PDA is the result of ADHD combining with autism was suggested in online forums before the term AuDHD was popularized. As stated in the ADHD section at the start of this chapter, our experience is that AuDHD people who aren't also PDA don't experience PDA's hallmark irrational avoidance.

We've noticed as well that AuDHD culture often "assumes" that PDA traits, such as expectations triggering avoidance, are nuances of ADHD. However, these supposed nuances aren't part of the diagnostic criteria for ADHD.[31] It's true that AuDHD makes people prone to avoidance. Autistic people who aren't PDA may become extremely avoidant for many reasons, including sensory overload. This is covered in more detail later in this section, under "extreme demand avoidance (EDA)." ADHD-specific avoidance tends to be rooted in focus ability. However, PDA brains can be totally focused on a task they are avoiding because it feels like a demand.

Many AuDHD people report trauma from neurotypical expectations that they've been unable to meet. Over time, compounded trauma can cause certain demands to become triggering. Although this can coincide with PDA avoidance, our "brand" of avoidance can strike at newly encountered demands that no one has asked us to meet. It also shows up in children who are too young to have experienced the level of trauma necessary to explain the scope of their avoidances.

For example, we may be out strolling in the countryside and develop an instant and overwhelming aversion, or irrational attraction to, a thorn bush we've never seen before. The threat response is triggered, prompting the PDA person to steer irrationally towards or away from the unfamiliar bush. We argue this example of avoidance is not rational, is not about focus ability, and is not about compound trauma. It doesn't benefit the individual and, in fact, can lead to them being spiked by thorns.

Another difference between ADHD and PDA is susceptibility to being coached. ADHD coaches exist because ADHD people benefit from coaching. But most PDA people don't—at least, not without a strong foundation of trust that can be time-consuming and expensive to achieve. Surface-level prompts and encouragement tend to have the opposite effect of triggering our demand avoidance to make us markedly less motivated than we were to begin with.

> **Sally:** When I first tried out ADHD medication, I suddenly became aware of things that needed cleaning in our kitchen and, to my surprise, I was enthusiastic to clean them. I'd never felt anything like this before. I thought I must have been mistaken about having been PDA. But then, after about

> 20 minutes, the novelty wore off and my brain started grumbling and whining that cleaning was "bad" and "boring" and that I should avoid it!

Bipolar disorder

Extreme mood swings

Bipolar's signifying mood shifts last for weeks at a time, but the roller-coaster emotions associated with PDA can switch multiple times during a single day.

> **Brook:** After my first major period of burnout in my early 30s, I was diagnosed bipolar type 2. This never sat right for me because I could sense that my erratic energy swings did have roots in events, such as feeling increasingly depressed and exhausted when I didn't have enough flexibility in my life. PDA finally made sense of this pattern where bipolar did not.

Burnout

Avoiding interaction with the world, avoiding tasks we normally enjoy

All people are prone to increased amounts of demand avoidance when exhausted, but PDA-type avoidance exists even if someone is highly supported and not drained. In fact, at our best we PDA people are only able to engage with life on our own terms.

Burnout is explored in detail in Chapter 8.

> **Brook:** Through my 20s, I assumed my PDA traits were because I was lazy and poorly parented, so I tried to push myself to do better. It only took three months for me to spiral downhill, and at the end of six months I had gained weight and was crying at the drop of a hat. Once I stopped working, it took me five years to slowly recover to where I could cautiously engage with the world again.

Complex post-traumatic stress disorder (CPTSD)

Anxiety, unpredictability and avoiding interaction with others

The high demand avoidance, anxiety, and emotional unpredictability associated with PDA parallel CPTSD, but don't have specific triggers linked to past traumas.

> **Brook:** Before knowing about PDA, I underwent years of therapy and medication, and conquered many of my complex traumas tied to relationships. It was my triggers with tasks that I could not figure out, though, and I resigned myself to being mysteriously broken before I learned about PDA.

Conduct disorder

Childhood rule-breaking, fibbing, antisocial behavior, and possible violence

Fibbing is associated with both conduct disorder and PDA, and both conditions are thought to be neurologically rooted. PDA, though, is marked by avoiding demands in socially creative ways, instead of outright refusal. Also, PDA encompasses the additional traits of liking novelty, role play, or fantasy, and having a high need for personal control.

Depression

Avoiding things we once enjoyed

Depression is an acquired mental health condition, whereas PDA is present from birth. Although PDA people may be less tolerant of perceived demands at certain times (e.g., if we're in burnout), our tendency to avoid enjoyable activities is constant.

> **Brook:** I can be completely content and still triggered by demands. Of course, if I'm also depressed, my PDA is even harder to navigate, but even in my happiest moments, I am swerving around triggers.

Emotional dysregulation

Roller-coaster emotions, impulsiveness, difficulty maintaining relationships

Emotional dysregulation is classed as a mental health symptom, rather than as a diagnosable disorder. It refers to having out-of-control feelings which impact what a person says and does. Signs of emotional dysregulation include anger outbursts, irritability, mood swings, impulsiveness, and difficulties with maintaining relationships.[32]

Unsupported PDA people may be prone to emotional dysregulation because of innate anxiety and control need. However, there's more to PDA than emotional and relationship difficulties. It pays to look beyond surface-level behaviors to find the root cause. If patterns of distress stem from PDA, there'll be core-level resistance to "everyday" demands (such as personal hygiene and/or arbitrary rules).

> **Dara:** My 14-year-old daughter has sadly been misdiagnosed up until now. She has been told how mean and selfish she is, how she doesn't care about anything unless it benefits her, how she cannot read the room, is inflexible, lazy, unkind. It has felt impossible to be her parent. Professionals have diagnosed her with emotional dysregulation disorder.
>
> Reading about PDA makes me feel like I am reading about my daughter. So specifically. It's unbelievable. It explains everything. I cannot imagine what it has been like to be her up until now. The family is trying hard to retrain ourselves to respond to her differently, to be more collaborative and more patient, and understanding of her negative behaviors.

Extreme demand avoidance (EDA)

Avoiding everyday demands to an extreme extent

Sometimes termed autistic or rational demand avoidance, EDA results from specific unmet needs.[33] For example, it's rational for a person who needs reduced stimulation to avoid going to a brightly lit store. Other triggers that can lead an autistic person to avoid things for rational reasons are having their familiar routine disrupted and difficulties with transition.

Beyond this, as autism is often poorly supported, there are a large number of autistics experiencing burnout and the extreme form of demand avoidance that goes with it. PDA people need a lot of flexibility, but EDA support can entail more reliability, stability, and predictability.

> **Brook:** While my desire to do the dishes in the same way stays constant, my attitude about doing them can fluctuate erratically. One day, I can feel good about doing them, but the next day, I feel terrified to do them because yesterday I did "well." This is internal pressure around my own expectations and not tied to anything external.

Fabricated or induced illness (FII)

Parents' explanations for their child's extreme behavior mismatches known causes

Previously called Munchausen syndrome by proxy, FII is a form of child abuse where a parent or carer exaggerates, or even causes, symptoms of illness in a child. It involves exaggerating symptoms, lying about health, or even poisoning the child, leading to unnecessary treatments or tests.

Sadly, the fact that so little is known about PDA has led educational and other professionals to misdiagnose children's PDA as parental FII. The results of this parent blaming can be catastrophic, and break vulnerable families apart at the hands of misguided social services.[34]

> **Danielle Jata-Hall:** As a single PDA parent, I have faced multiple allegations of FII over the years. In every situation, I have had to fight off these accusations with specialist help. I was even threatened with child protection, which prevented us from accessing the correct support. The fact that one of

my children already had PDA and ADHD diagnoses (from the NHS [the National Health Service in the UK) was disregarded, and social care, health, and education services joined forces to set an agenda in secret meetings to prove I was fabricating the needs of my family. This went on for months. I believe that professionals fundamentally lack an understanding of what PDA is, the support it requires, and knowledge of how it impacts the family. This creates a perfect recipe for parent blame. The repeated distress of the FII allegations never leaves families like ours and creates many extra threads of trauma to unravel.

Generalized anxiety disorder (GAD)

Excessive, uncontrollable anxiety that interferes with daily life

Generalized anxiety disorder (GAD) is characterized by persistent, overwhelming worry and anxiety that interfere with daily activities. Treatments such as psychotherapy, lifestyle changes, coping skills, and relaxation techniques can significantly improve symptoms and help individuals manage the condition.[35]

Although some of the techniques recommended for GAD may ease PDA anxiety, the difference is that PDA anxiety is inborn, not acquired, and therefore, can't be "cured."

Brook: As a young adult, I found jobs where I could do just enough to skate by. I was able to push myself at work for a while to not avoid things, then would sneakily avoid things but feel shame and guilt, and then it would almost always end up falling apart.

I sought help from a free clinic. I remember feeling anxious about feeling anxious. It was my first time trying to get help for all my struggles instead of hiding them. Feeling observed and "judged," even if it was to help me, was excruciating! The anxiety I described was attributed to general anxiety disorder, without a real explanation for *why* I was so anxious. I continued to flounder until I discovered my PDA.

Nonverbal learning disorder (NVLD)

Missing social cues without matching the traditional model of autism

NVLD impacts nonverbal learning, such as pattern matching, math concepts, and reading social cues. As NVLD doesn't affect memorizing spelling or rote learning, it tends not to be spotted until fifth grade when curricula require children to demonstrate conceptual thinking.[36]

> **S from Pennsylvania:** A few months after the initial misdiagnosis of ODD (see next section), I learned a tiny bit about PDA, but not enough, and brought the idea to the next person we went to, seeking better diagnoses. He clearly didn't know anything about PDA so did a standard autism evaluation and determined she didn't qualify, but diagnosed her with nonverbal learning disorder. While it sort of sounded like some of what we knew about our eight-going-on-nine-year-old, it didn't really help or give us any insight on how to better support her. Only PDA has helped us understand the reasons behind what often felt like explosions over nothing, and therefore helped us understand and support our child better.

Oppositional defiant disorder (ODD)

Resisting doing what parents and teachers ask

ODD involves a consistent pattern of angry, irritable moods, argumentative or defiant behavior, and a tendency to deliberately annoy or disobey authority figures.[37] ODD entails resisting specific things only, whereas PDA avoidance latches onto anything. Traditional parenting strategies tend to work for ODD, but don't for PDA. ODD is characterized by an outright refusal to comply, whereas PDA is characterized by using creative avoidance strategies.

ODD is possibly an overused catch-all explanation for childhood aggression. However, we think it's possible for a traumatized non-PDA child to exhibit surface-level PDA behaviors. If so, their aggression would be centered on the people or institutions that triggered their trauma. PDA-type avoidance affects our own desires and encompasses more than aggression.

> **Anonymous:** We had two different psychiatrists slap an ODD diagnosis on our PDAer at different times; one at age seven and the other at age eleven. The first doctor had only met my child for about 30 minutes, and the second one had never met them in person. That doctor spent about 5 minutes on a video call with my (avoidant) child—and about 20 minutes talking with me. Neither psychiatrist would entertain the idea of autism when I mentioned my concerns because my PDAer was "too social," "makes decent eye contact," and "has strong conversational skills" (none of which should have disqualified them from an autism evaluation or diagnosis). They latched onto ODD simply based on a description of avoidant distress behavior, which they perceived as willful defiance.

PANS and PANDAS

Separation anxiety, moodiness, anxiety, and becoming obsessive

Because of the complexity of PANS (pediatric acute-onset neuropsychiatric syndrome)/PANDAS (pediatric autoimmune neuropsychiatric disorders associated with streptococcal infections) and the higher rate of co-occurrence with PDA, it is beyond the scope of this book to detail all the unique presentations of the condition. More information is available at www.pandasppn.org.

As a general summary, however, PANS/PANDAS behavior "flares" are often triggered by environmental factors such as mold and toxins, and are said to subside with anti-inflammatory medication. They do not entail creative avoidance strategies, nor are they alleviated in the long term by low-demand supports, which are hallmarks of PDA.

> **Libby Hill, Small Talk Speech and Language Therapy:** Anna, aged six, was referred to me because of concerns about PDA. She had frequent meltdowns at home, but good behavior in

> school. Her school saw no issues and blamed the mother for not being firm enough. When her mother applied for an EHCP [education, health, and care plan in the UK], I was called to assess her language and communication because of my experience with PDA. Initially, Anna resisted, but eventually allowed me to speak with her mother. During the assessment, Anna showed severe mood shifts, becoming aggressive toward her mother, using violence and shouting. Using low-arousal strategies, I completed the assessment. Anna later received a PANS/PANDAS diagnosis from a private pediatrician, and after treatment, she returned to her usual self and entirely stopped being violent towards her mother.

PERSONALITY DISORDERS

Personality disorders are entrenched mental health conditions that affect how people think, feel, behave, and relate to others. It's possible that some unsupported PDA individuals meet the criteria for personality disorder diagnosis if their maladaptive way of coping has become fixed. Personality disorders are defined by external behaviors, not the underlying cause. This means that although a dysregulated PDA person may meet all the criteria for personality disorder diagnosis, the standard treatment plan will be ineffective. PDA people report having been diagnosed with a variety of personality disorders.

Avoidant and other personality disorders

Insecure social connection, avoidance rooted in anxiety about rejection

There are many ways in which unrecognized PDA might be interpreted as a personality disorder. As we saw in Chapter 1, PDA is characterized by roller-coaster emotions, social difficulties that may mismatch our ability to use charm and eye contact, and an overarching tendency to avoid seemingly random things, often to our own detriment.

Hemmel Mol: After graduating, I had difficulty keeping a job. I decided I must be the cause of this. I asked my therapist to get me committed to a mental institution where a friend of mine had been an inpatient. My diagnosis, after weeks of observation, was personality disorder not otherwise specified. They saw signs of avoidance, narcissism, and dependency. I lived together with 42 other clients for six months, in a facility that specialized in social behavioral problems. It was hard, but I learned how to behave so nobody would think I was weird, ever again—for example, sitting next to people I liked, and looking strangers in the eyes.

When I told the staff I lied and manipulated them, they told me to leave at the end of the week. I was glad because the other patients disliked me, and I felt hindered by them in my attempts to try out new behavior.

This experience taught me that manipulation and lies are a big no-no. It took me years to learn this, but I am honest now. I had a very good relationship with my GP, who asked me to see a psychiatrist. I had one meeting and got the diagnosis paranoid personality disorder and an anti-anxiety prescription. But my mental health issues continued.

I recently met an old friend who told me she had autistic burnout. This was a revelation for me. I scored high on autism screenings my psychologist carried out. When I came across PDA, it described me very accurately. I am convinced the personality disorders that people diagnosed were traits of my PDA.

Borderline personality disorder (BPD)

Volatile emotions, neediness, and reckless behavior

Sometimes called emotionally unstable personality disorder, BPD and PDA may appear similar on the surface, but borderline personality disorder doesn't entail an extra layer of irrational demand avoidance.[38] Many people think BPD is a stigmatizing label applied to neurodivergent people who are over-stressed from trying to fit into a world designed for neurotypicals.

PDA people seem prone to developing BPD-like traits when social focus overrides wariness.

> **Sally:** I retrospectively diagnosed myself with BPD when I first came to suspect my autism. My messy, younger self ticked all the qualifying boxes for BPD, but I later realized that it had resulted from unsupported PDA causing my emotions to swing so far off kilter that I'd been unable to cope at all.

Narcissistic personality disorder (NPD)

Fragile self-esteem, criticism of others, seeking unusual accommodations, fantastical worldview, reliance on others to confirm self-worth

Although there may be superficial similarities, NPD doesn't entail that extra layer of irrational demand avoidance. NPD might involve someone processing intense emotions by casting blame and being dependent on other people for affirmation. When a parent has NPD, they might use their child as a scapegoat or look to them for praise.[39]

> **Sally:** I've lost count of the number of fellow PDA adults who've said their parent, or some other close family member, is NPD. From personal experience, I suspect these family members are actually PDA too, but using protective narcissism as a malfunctioning defense strategy.

Separation anxiety

Severe anxiety about being separated from a caregiver that can last into adulthood

Separation anxiety is common in young children, but it tends to ease by age 2–3. If the anxiety is particularly intense, lasts beyond toddler years, or disrupts daily life, it may indicate separation anxiety disorder.[40] Separation anxiety disorder can affect teens and adults, causing difficulty leaving home or work.

Although social anxiety is common for PDA people, it occurs

alongside other hallmark traits, such as using creative and/or social strategies to avoid everyday demands.

> **Brook:** Most of my kids struggle with being apart from me, and I've been accused of encouraging this (without evidence). I'm actually very present but laid-back as a parent, but my kids have still struggled with being apart from me in ways some people consider age-inappropriate. Besides sometimes getting overwhelmed (I am the opposite and need time to myself to recharge), I don't shame them for needing this, but try to think of ways to reassure them that they can reach me whenever they need to.

CHAPTER 5

PDA Positives

The good news is that many positives come with PDA. Few of these positives are included in traditional traits lists, because PDA was first identified by clinicians and theorists whose perception was limited to children whose disruptive behaviors drew their attention. PDA positives have been revealed by discussions within the PDA community, both between parents and carers of PDA kids, and between PDA adults. These include having a good sense of humor and being creative.

PEER RESEARCH RESULTS

PDA positives—like creativity and humor—are often talked about by people with lived experience of PDA, such as members of online support forums, but are not included in traditional traits lists. When, in 2018, Sally Cat invited parents and carers to put forward three positive words to describe their PDA kids, 40 percent said "funny," and 19 percent said "creative." Other commonly given words were: caring, intelligent, bright, talented, charming, determined, and unique.

In 2016, Sally Cat sought to remedy the scarcity of academic attention to the broader spectrum of PDA traits, including positive ones, by coordinating a large peer study to determine whether 155 potentially unique PDA traits, which had been suggested by fellow PDA adults, were shared with the general autistic community. The rankings of 105 traits showed a statistically significant difference between PDA and general autistic participants, with PDA people having scored themselves more highly in each instance. The quotes at the beginning of each trait description below are ones that showed a significant difference for PDA compared to general autism; they are from Sally Cat's peer study (see ADHD in Chapter 4).

POSITIVE PDA TRAITS

Humor

> "I have a fantastic sense of humor."
> "People misunderstand my friendly sarcasm and are sometimes upset."
> "I am prone to hyper behavior/silliness."

PDA kids, as well as adults, are often described as having a good sense of humor. It varies from person to person, but our PDA humor may be quirky and, sometimes, very dark. This brand of humor can make others feel weirded out. Similarly, if we have a sarcastic humor style, we may offend people without meaning to.

There's a likelihood that PDA people will be hyper and silly from time to time. An extreme form of this is funster (see Chapter 3), but we can be silly and hyper without major panic driving us. When this happens, ludicrous things feel absolutely hilarious. It may be sparked by the giddy joy that comes from rebelling against life's constant onslaught of demands to conform and deport ourselves correctly. It can be a huge relief to stop trying for a moment and stick our proverbial two fingers up at the world in general.

PDA humor, coupled with our inclination to adapt our communication to put others at ease, can be uplifting to the people we come into contact with, especially if we're relaxed and reactive, as opposed to being in a panicked funster mode that can make those around us feel on edge.

> **Brook:** My kids' sardonic humor is their most obvious trait. They find dark humor enjoyable in a way that most kids don't appreciate, and I can laugh with them about jokes that usually only jaded adults can appreciate!

Creativity

> "I am imaginative/creative."
> "I had a rich fantasy world, which I preferred to reality."
> "I experience vivid dreams."

Creativity is another positive trait that PDA people are often described as having. Our PDA brains seem to have a natural tendency to think outside the box and come up with unexpected ideas that surprise others.

Our creativity is, perhaps, unsurprising in light of the barrage of things our brains have compelled us to avoid, avoid, avoid since the moment of our birth. PDA creativity might, therefore, be the result of endlessly pushing our mental capacity to its limits to find strategies to avoid the random things our brains command us to avoid. Our propensity to role play could be thought of as part of this.

But it might not be so simple. PDA creativity appears to be connected to experiencing things with unusual intensity. We've already seen that PDA is associated with having super-strong emotions, but we may experience other things very intensely, too—for example, by reveling in visual patterns, or by being sensitive to auditory matches, like similar sounds, which others don't notice.

As we'll see in the next chapter, some PDA babies seem primed to trance out. However, this might stem from a co-occurring condition, such as sensory processing disorder, and not in actuality be inherent to PDA. It's impossible to know for certain until more research is carried out.

Creativity is an invaluable asset to our society—without it, nothing would be invented, and better solutions wouldn't be found. PDA people might not be good at working 9–5, but we can make valuable contributions to our communities and the wider world if doors are opened for us to work in our own quirky and ultra-creative ways.

> **Brook:** My brain thrives on thinking outside the box. Whenever I find a hobby, I immediately think of unexpected ways to apply ideas. Like a few years back, I was hyperfocused on indoor plants, and there were a few times I had ideas that I couldn't implement because of my burnout, but that I saw also conceived of and marketed by others later.

Verbal ability

> "My verbal ability may disguise my lack of processing speed."

PDA people may have verbal skills that are much faster than our mental processing speed. In fact, our verbal communication may be so good that observers believe us to be completely on the ball when in reality our brains are slower than our tongues, and it can take us a good while to process what's been said to us. This mismatch between verbal ability and processing speed is similar to pain-masking behavior (see Chapter 2) because, in both cases, our underlying weakness is disguised.

A parent's belief that their child is struggling socially or academically may be dismissed if the child in question is highly articulate and socially clever. Autism diagnoses can be refused, and learning difficulties can be denied.

> **Brook:** I am highly adept at absorbing how others are speaking around me and naturally fold it into my persona that I present with them. This adept social mirroring and verbal charm that I do not cognitively think through was a big reason why it took me a long time to absorb that it was possible for me to be autistic.

Word play

> "I make up new words to replace common words."
> "I make up new names for people."
> "I mispronounce words deliberately."
> "I make odd noises."

Word play is perhaps the most fun PDA trait, although some might find it annoying. PDA word play includes inventing new words for common objects and new names for people and pets. It can also involve deliberately mispronouncing words or making peculiar, nonverbal sounds.

Not all PDA people are drawn to word play, but, from anecdotal experience, some experienced diagnosticians recognize it as a telltale signifier. PDA word play seems to have a light-hearted, friendly intent, but, like our well-intended sarcasm, others might not appreciate being on the receiving end of, for example, being given a new name or listening to endless puns.

The underlying driver may be a fusion of PDA creativity and demand avoidance against using expected vocabulary. Inventing new words and names, or mispronouncing established ones, gives a little of that personal control that we PDA people need so badly.

Renaming a person gives us control of their identity. Renaming a food—for example, calling dauphinoise potatoes "dolphin-nosed"—magics it from mundanity into a fun thing that we invented for ourselves. Similarly, mispronouncing the word "toothpaste" as "tithe-post" takes away the inherent demand of it having been predefined by someone else.

Having a natural inclination for word play can distinguish great poets, lyricists, and prose writers from wannabes. There's a pitfall, though: if you tell PDA people we're great at something, the chances are that we'll never do it again because your praise, no matter how well intentioned, carries demand pressure for repeat performances. Issues with praise are explored further in Chapter 7.

> **Brook:** Whenever my brother and I interact, we have our own accent that has now spread to his daughter (my niece). I didn't even notice it until my ex pointed out how I always talk funny when I'm interacting with that side of my family! There was also a time that my niece's boyfriend came to visit, and he later revealed it made him uncomfortable that we all immediately gave him a nickname.

Social ability

> "I like to communicate."
> "I copy tone of voice and accents, trying to 'fit in' to social circles."
> "I can be charming."
> "I get confused as to why people tell me I am manipulative."

Enjoying communicating with others seems to be a hallmark of PDA that's tied in with our inherent social focus. As we saw in Chapter 2, we may choose to adapt our interaction style to put the person or people we're communicating with at ease, and that doing this helps us gain the outcomes we want (e.g., succeeding in a job interview). It's worth reiterating that this is different from the abusive form of imposed masking that autistic people talk of dropping. Unlike imposed masking, voluntary adaptive communication can be thought of as a positive behavior that benefits all parties.

A lot of PDA adults say they've been described as manipulative and that this has confused them. PDA is associated with having social communication difficulties, so if a PDA person uses adaptive communication to compensate for this, then they're not being manipulative in the sense that they're not sneakily trying to gain power. Instead, they're trying to equalize things.

It is worth noting too that, at a simpler level, if the term "manipulation" means actively participating in how an outcome is achieved, this is something everyone does. Having said this, some PDA people may indeed use charm to manipulate others in the darker, power-stealing sense of the word. We explore abuse and vulnerability to abuse in Chapter 9.

> **Sally:** I was truly surprised when a previous boyfriend accused me of being manipulative. I'd felt so clueless and powerless in our fractious relationship that the thought of me manipulating it was laughable.

Unconventional solutions

> "I can come up with unconventional solutions that surprise people."
> "I like trying to get to the bottom of how things work, especially people/social things."
> "I am logical rather than emotional: I analyze myself, other people, and social situations."

Another common PDA positive is coming up with off-the-wall ideas and solutions that nobody else has thought of. This can be seen as an offshoot of our creativity and, perhaps, our tendency to quibble against the established ways of doing things.

We seem naturally inclined to analyze our worlds to make sense of how things, social interactions, and other people work. This might be because our control-needing brains can't cope with uncertainty.

A 2019 study by the University of Newcastle found that intolerance of uncertainty was ultra-high for PDA kids.[1]

All of this benefits society because positive progress can't happen unless people come up with fresh ideas and challenge established ways of doing things. Our PDA tendency to quibble may be very annoying from time to time, but it has the potential to change the world, too!

> **Sally:** I've never been content to be a surface-level tourist. I've always wanted to get to the roots of things, so I know how they work and, more importantly, understand the hearts of the people who make these things work.

Passion

> "I develop attachments to particular places."
> "I like to hear the same songs/watch the same TV show/read the same book series."
> "I am not motivated by money, but will work for hours unpaid, so long as there is no demand that I do this."

We PDA people experience things very intensely. Our emotions plunge from high to low like a roller coaster. Our demand avoidance can turn us stone-cold against something, or someone, but we have fire in us, too. Without it, we'd never get anywhere, because we'd never fight our demand avoidance's constant vetoes. We operate on a knife-edge between demand-avoidant inertia and counterbalancing impassioned tenacity. No wonder we need so much recharge time!

Our passion can propel us into the agony of limerence (people obsession), but take us to joyous places, too. We can fall in love with particular places and particular tunes or TV shows. As with limerence, any of these things can become unbearably intense, but when they don't burn us, they enrich our worlds.

Demand avoidance may stop us from working at someone else's command, but our passion drives us to work, for long hours, without demanding or wanting any payment. The projects of our passion tend to be flavored by our social focus, so they involve helping others or our community.

> **Brook:** I will (and have!) worked thousands of hours as a volunteer on many projects. Volunteering my time helps me feel like I keep expectations reasonable and the perception of demands lower, and I don't feel like I'm measuring my outcome to be sure that it warrants whatever payments I receive when I do traditional work. As soon as I accept money for that same exact work, it almost always completely cripples me from completing it.

Compassionate empathy

> "I like to help people."
> "I am empathic (feel empathy)."
> "I can give the impression of having no empathy."

When asked to give three positive words to describe their PDA kids, "compassion" and "empathy" were often chosen. Despite the stereotype that autistic people have no empathy, the three traits listed above are common for autistic people, as opposed to being specific to PDA.[2] Perhaps surprisingly, PDA people were more likely to believe they came across as unempathetic. This could be because of our tendency to adapt our communication so we come across well to others.

The empathy we feel can be overwhelming—for example, feeling crushed by somebody else's misfortune. We can be hypersensitive to emotional atmospheres when we enter a room. On the other hand, our burning compassion can be fueled by false empathy, such as being panicked that a friend can't cope with having no dollars to see them through to payday when the friend in question is actually totally chilled.

Who, or what, we empathize with can be very arbitrary. We might be brought to tears by someone's imagined plight while simultaneously being unmoved by another person's genuine ordeal. The latter can come about because the other person's neediness triggers our demand avoidance, so we object to the idea of helping them.

> **Sally:** I can get horrifically distressed by imagining another person's suffering. I can't bear the thought of them struggling with things I've gone through. On some occasions, I've bombarded people with help they haven't wanted. For example, when someone told me they couldn't afford tobacco, I gave them my emergency bag of half-smoked, hand-rolled cigarettes.

Social equalizing drive

> "I understood fairness from an early age."
> "I hate injustice."
> "Respect and trust are important to me."
> "I may leap to the rescue of a person or animal being abused."

Our social equalizing drive is another PDA plus that seems common. We have a tendency to champion underdogs, be they an animal in distress, a bullied classmate, or a vulnerable minority whose plight has come to our attention.

This is where our questioning of arbitrary hierarchy and quibbling shines forth as fighting repression. If we notice people or animals being treated unfairly, we may charge to their rescue like superheroes who will fight for good, regardless of the danger to ourselves. Think of a mama bear protecting her cubs: nobody sane wants to mess with this level of totally committed, self-sacrificing wrath! We follow our own codes of ethics and, because of this, question things that many non-PDA people blindly accept.

Although our social equalizing drive might make us seem saint-like, it's often a knee-jerk reaction to hearing criticism of someone else. People who've spent time in adult PDA forums may have witnessed people jumping to defend someone who's not even in the group simply because a fellow member said they have an issue with them. For example, if a married PDA person makes a post about problems with their spouse, people may irrationally argue on the spouse's behalf in place of offering support to their already distressed fellow group member. So, in this light, our equalizing drive isn't concerned with assessing facts. In fact, our social equalizing drive doesn't make us immune to holding prejudiced views. A PDA man, for instance, may be a misogynist, or a white PDA person may be a racist.

Our PDA drive for social equality is sometimes referred to as a "sense of justice," but we consider this problematic because it gives the false impression that we're aware of all aspects of justice, which can be distressing for victims. For example, if a prominent person, who is known to have abused women, is described as having a good sense of justice, the message is that the harm they inflicted is of no consequence.

We're also not immune to being suckered in by charlatans. PDA people are often, if not always, socially naïve, and this can cause us to miss crucial clues that someone has a hidden agenda, especially if our social equalizing drive has got us ramped up to rescue them from an imagined injustice—and, worse still, if we've developed limerence (an obsession) about them. We explore vulnerability to abuse in Chapter 9.

Sometimes, however, our social equalizing drive can serve as a phenomenal force for good, which leads us to stand up, alone, to face genuine injustice that no one else calls out.

> **Sally:** When my best friend was in crisis, I could tell that her other friends were annoyed with me for arguing about her cat's needs when they were arranging for her to move into one of their houses which had a big, hectic dog living there.

Self-exploration

> "I have found that learning to suspend judgment and let it go is helpful."
>
> "I have my own set of ethics that do not necessarily correspond to society's, the law, etc."
>
> "I am open-minded: more liberal, more willing to hear all sides, less judgmental."

There seem to be lots of PDA adults who are keen to work out who they are and what makes them tick. This is a logical offshoot of our tendency to see things in new ways that stems from our intolerance of uncertainty (described above). As well as this, we may want to explore who we are because we're confused by our failure to match social expectations. For example, if everyone around us, including our close family and friends, expects us to flourish as an employee, we'll likely be very confused if the reality of having a job is unendurable.

It's also worth bearing in mind that the reason self-exploration appears to be a common PDA trait might be because PDA people who aren't into exploring themselves have no interest in seeking out PDA communities and fly under the radar.

No matter how common self-exploration is to PDA people, when present it's a hugely positive trait because it guides us to navigate through the confusion of our clashing drivers, which comprise our basic needs; our irrational demand avoidance; our roller-coastering, super-intense emotions, including anxiety; and our drive to fit and get along with others. Having an additional driver that leads us to explore ourselves steers us from being trapped in the lose-lose mindset of scapegoating.

> **Sally:** I dedicated decades of my confused, misfitting adult life to working out why I kept on failing to integrate with society and kept making social blunders, which crushed me to my soul. Making sense of who I was felt like trying to unravel a massive knot of tangled strings. The more I've come to understand myself, the happier and stronger I've become.

It's clear then that many good traits come with being PDA, and that these positives are extensions of PDA's core traits of entrenched demand avoidance, control need, and people focus. These combine to make us question long-standing assumptions and be moved by compassion to aid others whom we perceive as crushed by society's thoughtless injustice.

CHAPTER 6

Babyhood and Toddlerhood

This chapter takes an in-depth look at how, with hindsight, parents recognize signs of PDA in babies and very young children. We suggest strategies for easing infant stress, resistance, and anxiety. Dr. Judy Eaton, who runs a clinic in England that specializes in PDA, states that diagnosis of PDA is only possible where there's "demand avoidance that has been present since early infancy and presented across contexts and time, often beginning with the child demonstrating reluctance to comply with daily tasks such as nappy (diaper) changes [or] being placed in a car seat."[1]

The quotes at the start of each PDA trait description in this chapter were originally collected in 2020 from members of a Facebook group called Free PDA.

PRE-BIRTH PDA

> "My daughter was 13 days overdue, positioned sideways and wouldn't budge. She needed a hell of a lot of persuasion to come out!"

> "He broke his waters at 32 weeks, and the doctors joked that he was a stroppy little monkey... As soon as he was born he was absolutely fine. The doctor said you're going to know you've got that one!"

Plenty of parents will tell you that their PDA kids showed marked signs of resistance before they were even born. It might be hard to imagine that a tiny, helpless, wholly inexperienced fetus could be actively avoidant. Surely, unborn babies are guided only by survival instincts, such as hunger for milk and being attracted to human faces?

Some people have speculated that PDA is "caused" by birth trauma, implying that our PDA traits aren't natural to us and are, instead, the infant equivalent of CPTSD (complex post-traumatic stress disorder). However, there have been many first-hand accounts of PDA babies being born easily without trauma. Additionally, if PDA is a lifelong condition, it's something we're born with. This means we were already PDA as fetuses.

There is no empirical evidence, of course, but anecdotal evidence for pre-birth PDA abounds in first-hand accounts, like the ones given here:

> **Brook:** My oldest tried coming out face-first presentation so I had to get a C-section.

> **Sally:** I've got a photo of my daughter cradled in my arms seconds after her delivery by C-section because she'd jammed herself into a position from which a natural birth was impossible. She looks absolutely furious!

PASSIVE PDA BABIES

> **Philippa:** By a couple of months old, our son was sleeping 7pm–10am and napping 12pm–2pm. It felt like I hardly saw him awake. He was difficult to wake up. When he was awake, he was the most chilled baby. Hit all his milestones early. He didn't seem to need anything until he started preschool at 18 months old. Then he changed overnight.

Researchers have noted that many children matching the PDA profile were passive during babyhood.[2] It stands to reason that if a baby is placid, no one's going to suspect PDA unless there's both a reason to—for example, if older siblings are PDA—and knowledge that PDA can present passively in infants. For this reason, PDA is often picked up when the child is older and baby passivity is noted retrospectively.

No one knows for sure why it is that PDA babies are often passive, but one reason could be that as infants have everything done for them, they're blissfully untroubled by demands until they reach toddlerhood. Another potential reason for the passiveness of some PDA babies is demand avoidance against parents wanting them to hit milestones. After all, the easiest way to avoid a parent's expectations is to not do it.

> **Alana Neimanis:** I thought my son couldn't sit up by the age of eight months old and was so worried until I realized, while leaving him alone in his cot and watching from the door semi-closed, that he could sit up perfectly; he would just not do it on command!

Trancing out

Some passive PDA babies appear to be deeply moved by sensory stimuli, whether it's the feel of strong wind, shafts of light, patterns, bright colors, rhythmic sounds, strong tastes, or anything else that absorbs their infantile attention.

Glimpses into tiny PDA minds can be gained, retrospectively, by adults in possession of a rare form of synesthesia—known as time-space or calendar—that stores memories from infancy. Sally Cat has vivid memories from when she was six months old. Another PDA adult with vivid early memories recalls loving wall patterns cast by light through their bedroom curtains:

> **Miranda Jacobs:** I have a strong memory of the light coming through my bedroom curtains and making patterns on the wall... Also I really liked the wind—turning my pram into the wind would calm me.

Sensory immersion is, therefore, a third possible explanation for why PDA babies can be passive: we're just so wowed by all the brand-new sensory joys filling our lives that demands don't burst our bliss-filled baby bubbles. This tallies with the PDA traits of loving novelty and having deep perception, which, in Chapter 5, we linked to our PDA creativity, postulating that our brains are primed to experience things with heightened intensity.

> **Sally:** I have clear memories of being a baby and going into ecstasy over scenery things like colors and the repetitive roar of waves crashing on the pebble beach I was squatting on.
>
> My daughter, as a newborn, fixated on beams of light shining through our thick bedroom curtains. She was also transfixed by a colorful mobile we had hanging in the living room.
>
> She hated the outside world for her first few months and screamed every time I tried to take her outside, but later came to love the feel of wind on her face.

Masking

> **Maggie:** As she started to move about a bit, she often worked quietly under the radar while her more boisterous siblings would be taking center stage... She was always really shocked to find that I knew what she was up to, and still is now. Clearly thinks she's invisible.

There are parental accounts of PDA babies using both of the instinctive types of masking described in Chapter 2: adaptive communication and pain-masking behavior. Pain masking in babies can take the form of not crying when hurt or, in the example quoted above, silently pushing themselves forward without seeking any help from the adult who's caring for them. Adaptive communication in babies can express itself as using smiles and other social skills to charm adults and win them over.

> **Brook:** Two of my three boys were charmers as babies. My eldest masked his pain so much that my sister commented that he had better self-control than most adults do.

CORE PDA TRAITS IN BABIES

> **Lucy Holt:** Her first word, at about six or seven months old, was "NO!"

PDA traits are easier to spot if the baby isn't passive. These are the core traits of PDA, as outlined in Chapter 1:

- pathological type demand avoidance
- high anxiety
- high control need
- interest in people
- fondness of novelty

- strong, changeable emotions
- using creative and/or social strategies to avoid demands
- role play
- not being bound by social hierarchy.

However, babies are, well, merely babies, so even with the most expressive little soul, there are limited ways in which their neurological differences can stand out. Also, the social complexities that face children and adults bypass babies. No one, for example, expects a baby to respect social hierarchies, and all babies display strong, changeable emotions.

How, therefore, can anyone say for certain that a baby is PDA because of how they act? The answer is that although no one can, we can make educated guesses based on awareness of the nature of PDA as an integrated neurological profile. This is a wordy way of saying that the more we understand what PDA is, the better able we are to recognize it.

It can also be hard for first-time parents to pick up telltale signs because they have no older children to compare their baby's behavior with. One mom illustrates how it was easier for her to recognize PDA in her second child:

> **Josie Louise Ward:** With my youngest, I was able to see PDA signs from very young as I already had experience with my older PDAer. When he was seven months old, he would instantly get extremely angry if we ever took something away from him (playing with something he shouldn't have). He would throw himself back in a tantrum and scream, and I remember being really surprised. Then continued the other signs like hating nappy (diaper) changes; [he] would fight getting into his car seat, pushchair (stroller), etc.

Pathological-style demand avoidance

We've seen examples of babies avoiding diaper changes and being put in car seats. Other examples are spitting out food during weaning, not taking an offered toy, throwing off hats, and twisting legs away when a carer's trying to dress them in pants or tights. It's important to gauge whether a baby's avoidance is of the pathological kind, or if there's a rational explanation. Food might be spat out because of its taste. A toy might be refused because of distraction. Hats might be thrown because a carer encouraged them to throw a toy ball. Legs might jiggle when mom or dad is trying to dress them simply because it's all so much fun.

However, PDA isn't just about demand avoidance, so if a baby is PDA, other traits, such as people focus and control need, will show up too.

> **Sally:** My daughter said words, and even the phrase "over there," before she was eight months-old, but didn't repeat them until she was way, way older (like three). My sense is that her brain vetoed her saying them again.

High anxiety

Anxious babies can be easily panicked about being left alone and/or frequently burst into tears with or without an obvious cause. All kinds of things can feel threatening to an anxiety-prone baby: loud noises, being taken outdoors, the sudden proximity of a stranger, passing shadows, an unusual smell... The list is endless, just as it can be endless for anxious adults.

It may be worth considering whether anything happened to cause a baby's chronic anxiety. Humans aren't typically born with high anxiety built in, except (perhaps) in the case of PDA. As we saw in Chapter 4, PDA presents similarly to complex post-traumatic stress disorder (CPTSD) but differs because it has no link with past trauma.

Another point to remember is that although signs of high anxiety may point to a baby being PDA, it's not a solid guarantee. Similarly, a lack of apparent anxiety doesn't rule PDA out.

> **Mandarin Snap:** My daughter was really jumpy as a baby; she would jump even when someone walked past her. Wouldn't

> let me leave her side for the first six months and always had extreme reactions of fear to animals.

High control need

Because PDA neurology is inborn, PDA babies have a hardwired instinct to control their personal environments regardless of their ability to achieve this. PDA babies can't speak commands or tell others what to do, but they can make the best of what limited means they have at their disposal. Control can take the form of grabbing a parent's face to make them look at something, or willing their bodies to do things that babies of their age aren't expected to accomplish.

> **Adira Restless:** My PDA son was different from the start. Everything had to be on his terms from day one. He forced himself upright in the hospital and shocked the nurses because they thought that was impossible.

Interest in people

The PDA trait of people focus can show up in babies. The examples given here are from a mom on the Free PDA website and this book's co-author, Brook. In both cases, the PDA baby they describe exhibited an unexpected level of social focus.

Beyond this, it's important to bear in mind that some PDA babies display less social focus than others.

> **Anonymous:** From the start, he was straining to hold his head up and look around. Health visitors commented on how strong he was and how intent he was on interacting with people.

Fondness of novelty

If a baby grabs for something new, it's a sure sign that they're interested in it. Other babyhood signs of liking novelty are smiling or shrieking happily when they're presented with new things.

> **Anonymous:** Constantly needed attention and new toys. Needed new stimuli. I would pick up a toy from the store, let him play with it while I shopped, and put it back when we were done, and he was all good.

Strong, changeable emotions

All babies are primed to cry a lot because it's their default way of communicating their needs. PDA babies, however, may cry more than others do, and as we've seen, they might be prone to high anxiety. They may also laugh a lot more than most babies do because both negative and positive emotions run strongly.

> **Jazz Spree:** Sometimes she would cry for no apparent reason, appear to be really cross or frustrated by our attempts to placate her (after checking the roll call of usual triggers, obviously). She would eventually wear herself out and sleep.

Using creative and/or social strategies to avoid demands

The concept of a baby using social strategies will likely seem nonsensical. However, the social strategizing that comes with PDA is more of a knee-jerk evasion tactic than anything that's been carefully thought through. In fact, the entire "pathological" nature of our avoidance is anything but rational. Therefore, there's a good possibility that preverbal PDA babies instinctively use their available range of social interaction techniques (grabbing, screaming, ignoring, etc.) to help them avoid whatever stuff their infant brains command them to.

> **Anonymous:** From about four months, she'd be in your arms and suddenly lunge her whole body away, so that she'd fall unless you moved to catch her.

Role play

The PDA trait of role play can be hard to spot in preverbal babies because they can't communicate their ideas. It's worth bearing in mind that role play is a complex behavior that necessitates awareness of our own identity in order to play at being someone or something else. Studies of infant development suggest that self-awareness doesn't develop until about the age of two.[3] However, neurodivergent development, by its very nature, can mismatch standardized research findings.

A parallel example is the formation of long-term memories, which, according to research, doesn't happen before the age of about four years.[4] Sally Cat, however, is blessed with a neurodivergent condition called calendar or time-space synesthesia,[5] which stores long-term memories from a far earlier age than predicted by mainstream research. This means that the likelihood of non-PDA babies not being able to carry out role play isn't necessarily the same for PDA babies, because they have different neurological wiring.

> **Jessica Fox:** I caught him practicing facial expressions, happy and sad, in front of a mirror when he was about 18 months old, and thought at the time that the ease at which he did so looked possibly manipulative or at the very least performative, like he had worked out a way to get what he wanted.

Not being bound by social hierarchy

The PDA trait of being unbound by social hierarchy is something people might think completely beyond a baby's ability to comprehend. But a PDA baby might reject hierarchical expectations at a fundamental level that's got nothing to do with the abstract concept of what hierarchy means. This might, for example, take the form of a baby lacking an instinct to presume that grownups know better than them, so, unlike non-PDA babies, they don't automatically defer to directions given by adults.

> **Adira Restless:** No one's ever been able to get her to do anything she didn't want to do. She started child care at one, and I very quickly got comments like "She's very stubborn, isn't she?"

> She has also always refused to wave or say hello or goodbye to people—instead turning her head away in a huff.

TODDLERHOOD YEARS

> **Anonymous:** He was very easygoing as a baby. When he hit three, it all changed!

Toddlerhood is the transition period between being a largely immobile, wordless baby to becoming a competently functioning miniature human being. A child's first toddling steps are a giant developmental leap into a new world of physical and linguistic ability. Thus empowered, toddlers can rebel against parental expectations by arguing back, running off, or, if all else fails, screaming in rage that any part of their life's new freedom has been denied to them. Hence, this period is dubbed "the terrible twos," although this type of rebellion can be delayed or never happen.

Of course, no two children are the same, including within the PDA population, and some young ones' toddler months are a hiatus of placid amenability.

It can be hard to differentiate PDA from the natural changes that all toddlers go through during their pre-kindergarten years. How can you tell if prolonged defiance is standard behavior or the result of PDA's roller-coasting emotions and demand avoidance? The signs can be subtle but, as for babies, detectable if we know what to look out for. Some of these signs are clearer indicators of PDA than others, such as situational mutism, which by its nature doesn't stand out at all and could be accounted for by another neurodivergent condition.

Another common thing many PDA toddlers do, or at least want to do, is co-sleeping with their parents (see Chapter 7).

> **Brook:** My kids' avoidances and mood swings became more obvious as they got older. Like my middle child not plugging in

> his tablet even if the cord was right next to him...inches away. I'd point it out a couple of times, but eventually his tablet would die, and he'd be a mess.

The more a little kid is able to say and do, the more etiquette they're expected to display. Pre-kindergarten children are expected to say "please," "thank you," "hello," and "goodbye," and do what they're told. The likelihood is, however, that young PDA kids will refuse to replicate good manners. Societal pressure to be polite can trigger PDA avoidance because these social expectations are demands.

PDA kids' failure to use polite words and/or obey orders can raise disgruntled brows among their extended families and the public at large. Parents of PDA kids can be judged as unforgivably lax and lacking in etiquette themselves for having failed to instill acceptable manners in their progeny.

> **Sally:** As a first-time parent, I thought it my duty to set firm boundaries with my daughter. So, one morning, I insisted she said "please" before I let her have her breakfast.
>
> She didn't.
>
> I knew she could say the word perfectly well, but she kept her mouth firmly closed. We were at a stalemate, because I thought that if I backed down, she'd not learn important boundaries. It went on for nearly an hour with me feeling increasingly awful with myself for effectively abusing her. I could sense her high tension and distress, but she just would not say please.
>
> In the end, I wrote "PLEASE" on a scrap of paper and offered it to her, telling her what it said and that if she passed it to me, it would count as her having said it. She passed it to me quick as a flash!
>
> I never demanded politeness from her again. She eventually said "thank you" of her own volition. This was about four years later.

Thankfully, there are tried and tested strategies for harmonizing life in PDA families, which we explore in Chapter 10 (spoiler alert: demanding that kids say "please" is not one of the strategies we recommend).

CHAPTER 7

Childhood

Content Warning: The section in this chapter "Invisible mental health crisis for PDA kids" mentions depression, self-harm, and suicidal thoughts.

By the age of three or four, children can walk and talk like little champs. But do they? Signs of PDA during childhood include saying their legs don't work and/or being totally silent (situationally mute) with people who aren't close family.

The anonymous quotes in this chapter are provided by members of a PDA social media group in the USA.

"My legs don't work"

PDA children use social strategies to avoid demands, such as distracting people and inventing excuses. A classic excuse is saying "my legs don't work."[1] However, there's debate about whether this actually is a made-up excuse because "F" adrenal reactions are known to make people's legs go floppy (see "flop" in Chapter 3), so they actually don't work. This raises the interesting possibility that PDA's hallmark irrational avoidance can cause physical impediments.

The reality may be that PDA kids do sometimes find that their legs don't work but, on other occasions, saying so might be a creative, PDA-generated excuse for avoiding a demand.

> **Sally:** When my dog corners me with treat-demanding eyes, I often find myself spouting ridiculous excuses to her about why I can't fetch her treats because, for example, my entire body is disintegrating, and the floor's now made of lava.

Co-sleeping

Lots of parents say that their PDA kids continue to co-sleep with them long after starting kindergarten. Co-sleeping is often, if not always, caused by fear of sleeping solo. In Western culture, it's customary to encourage babies to sleep alone in cribs in separate nursery rooms, but this isn't the case in other cultures where co-sleeping is considered healthy and normal.

From the infant's point of view, being alone in the dark will feel anything but safe. Millions of years of evolution have instilled terror of "monsters," such as leopards, that creep through the night hunting for weak prey, such as unguarded babies, that can neither run nor fight back. It all comes back to fight, flight, and freeze again. It's little wonder that PDA kids, with their naturally ramped-up anxiety levels, seem to have even more fear of being alone in the dark than other kids do.

Some parents say their PDA kid is able to cope with sleeping in their own bed if they have a pet, such as a large, friendly dog, sharing it with them.

> **Sally:** My daughter co-slept with us until she was 11. I never begrudged it because I empathized with her fear of being alone

> in the dark. I'd been exactly the same as a kid, and my parents' solution of forcing me to put up with sleeping alone didn't make my panic go. I used to lie there in abject terror of being killed by monsters.

Food avoidance

Pronounced food avoidance is termed "avoidant restrictive food intake disorder" (ARFID). It's often reported by parents and carers of PDA kids, as well as a bunch of us PDA adults who are very selective with what we feel OK eating. Reasons for avoiding food are varied and may include sensory issues (e.g., texture and taste), fear of contamination (which can be irrational), and demand pressure that we have to eat something, even if the pressure is self-generated. An example of this is having demand avoidance against eating fruit because it's good for us.

An effective strategy can be to calmly tell a PDA child of concerns about their nutrition and give them space to think of things they could eat, or drink, to make their diet more balanced. ARFID is also discussed in Chapter 4.

> **Brook:** My kids seem to take longer to decide on trying foods outside of their comfort zones. From around ages 4–8 they would stick to the same eight or nine foods (and same brands!), but at age nine, both my older kids decided on their own to start trying new things. Following their lead meant I didn't add any additional demands, which I believe helped them feel safe when they decided to try something new.

Screen time

It's common for PDA kids, and adults, to spend a lot of time staring at smartphones and other screens. Parents can worry because extended screen use is thought to be very unhealthy for children. However, screen use can be a vital way for PDA people to self-regulate and recover from overload, so that we don't melt down.

> **Sally:** Extended screen time is essential for me to self-regulate. I hardly ever melt down these days. I don't worry about the time my daughter spends watching YouTube because I know it's vital for her too.

Problems with praise

Disliking praise has been considered so common for PDA kids that the EDA-Q[2] (the first assessment scale published for PDA) down-scores children who like to be told they have done a good job.

The reality is more nuanced. PDA people do like to be told we're good at things, as long as praise is specific and not over the top. For example, being told that we're "great at art" can panic us because it carries demand pressure to continue being good at it. Being told we're just "super-duper great" in an over-the-top or patronizing way would probably make anyone cringe, but can feel especially icky to PDA people because it puts us in the spotlight (like unremitting eye contact). However, specific praise, such as "I really like how you've drawn that" doesn't pressure us to live up to future standards of greatness.

> **Sally:** My daughter actually loves being praised for what she's done, just as I do. But I'm conscious to tread carefully when giving her praise because if I'm too full-on, she'll panic and not want it.

SCHOOL AND PDA

Western childhood is dominated by having to go to school. Unfortunately, school and PDA are almost always a bad fit. Reasons may include the education system's demand for compliance, suppression of individuality, and adherence to imposed routines. Demands inherent in school systems include:

- arriving as scheduled
- following dress codes

- following specific directions
- respecting hierarchy
- having no breaks without permission.

Beyond this, demand avoidance can alienate PDA kids from set topics. Signs of an internalizing PDA kid's struggles may be too subtle for education professionals to detect. Masking vulnerability can, and does, stop kids asking for help. Compliant straight-A students may suddenly break down and be unable to leave their bedrooms for years.

> During my daughter's lunch, which they eat in the classroom, she sat down at the table and immediately dumped her lunch on the floor. The teacher asked her to clean it up. She did not. Instead, she went to the teacher's desk, swiped everything off of it, and then sat on the top of her desk, grabbed the teacher's lunch, and proceeded to eat it while sitting on top of her desk.

Effective PDA strategies for educators

Although there's no magic wand to remove all the problems PDA kids face in mainstream education, teachers and support staff can help if they:

- tailor support to the individual child (e.g., an internalizing PDA kid might panic if given obvious special treatment)
- offer flexibility and choice
- explain the purpose of non-negotiable rules
- use non-demanding language (e.g., "We'll be having lunch soon" in place of "Get ready for lunch")
- recognize that challenging behaviors are involuntary and anxiety-based
- adapt the system (instead of coercing the child)
- learn the child's triggers so they can be preempted with appropriate support (e.g., if queuing for the library triggers them, take them there ahead of the class to help set up)

- monitor stress levels to reduce pressures before overload or meltdown
- stay calm, which helps the child stay calm too
- enable access to quiet space
- give advance notice of changes so the child doesn't feel out of control.

Supported or not, there are many elements of school systems that clash with PDA.

Fight adrenal response

Traditional descriptions of PDA tell of kids whose default response to stress is to fight—for example, by hitting and/or kicking classmates or staff—which can have serious repercussions, including being excluded from school.

> My son did all of seven days of public school before being kicked out for physical violence. He yelled and hit his aide, so they got the woman who runs the special education placement to escort him to the gymnasium, where an obstacle course was set up, which he knocked down and destroyed. By the time they finally called me to pick him up, he was corralled like an animal in a vestibule surrounded by teachers holding 6-foot-tall wrestling mats.

Flight adrenal response

If a kid's default adrenal response is flight, stress will cause them to try to escape classrooms and even the entire school.

> My six-year-old son most often uses flight as his way to escape, or gain control in school. He elopes from his classroom often, one time even leaving the school's front door. Admin believes that this is "behavior" and can be fixed with traditional methods of discipline.

Masking

A lot of PDA kids mask in school. It's important for educators to realize that PDA can present in children as being quiet, straight-A, model students. This can cause problems because, first, school staff might not notice if the child is struggling. Second, if a parent tells them that their child is unruly at home, they can presume they're a bad parent, or making things up, because the child in question is perfectly well behaved in school.

> **Sally:** When my daughter started school, she used to chew her cuffs to shreds and wet herself every day, but she never admitted to being anxious. Luckily, her school was understanding and watched out for her.

Friendship problems

The PDA traits of needing control and being sociable but lacking depth of understanding, such as missing social nuances, show up in the EDA-Q and include two issues which directly impact a child's ability to maintain healthy friendships: "Social interaction has to be on his or her own terms" and "Tells other children how they should behave, but does not feel these rules apply to him/herself."[3]

> My nine-year-old has only had a handful of play dates and birthday party invitations in her life. Sometimes there is miscommunication, and she feels angry and rejected. That can lead to her having a negative fixation on a person: wanting revenge and calling them an enemy.

Bullying

Bullies pick on kids who stand out as different, are too weak to fight back, and have nobody to protect them. Some PDA kids hit all these qualifiers because they fail to learn complex group behaviors that neurotypical children adopt at around the age of eight. It's a hard schoolyard reality that kids who haven't kept up with their peers' social development can be treated meanly and deliberately excluded.[4]

On the flip side, PDA children may become bullies themselves. In her memoir *Being Julia*, adult PDAer Julia Daunt says she was a school bully.[5] In forums, some PDA adults have shared that being a school bully gave them a buzz and made them feel powerful. In this sense, bullying might help a kid reclaim the vital sense of control that PDA folk need and school systems rob from them.

> **Sally:** Kids ganged up on me for being different. Girls I thought were friendly tricked me into saying the wrong thing, so I was, according to their unfathomable rules, cast out from them forever.
>
> I've had a lifelong fascination with fathoming the mysteries of how social interactions work, but I guess neurotypical kids just know it all automatically.

Petty crime

Petty crime, such as shoplifting and graffiti, is another way that unsupported PDA can sometimes express itself. This isn't to say that the majority of PDA kids are law-breakers, and if it happens, petty criminal behavior might begin later in life, but we've slotted it into the childhood section because anecdotally (and personally) we know that some PDA children break the law.

From a PDA perspective, laws are demands, and breaking them can return a sense of control to PDA youngsters who have been granted no control by society, including from parents and teachers who they're expected to obey unquestioningly.

> **Sally:** When I was eight, I started running wild with my friend by shoplifting and carrying out other petty crimes, like breaking into schools during holidays and throwing books around. It was exhilarating to break rules and run free.

Situational mutism and spare play

Situational mutism and spare play can be thought of as masking because they involve concealing vulnerability. Educators should be aware that a child's silence can be a sign of intense anxiety. As for masking in general, situationally mute kids are rarely able to ask for help. These conditions are explored in more depth in Chapter 2.

Schools not believing the child has an issue

A troubling number of parents say that schools either don't "believe in" PDA or assume their child can't be PDA because they behave perfectly well in school. Some schools resist using PDA strategies. This may be because these strategies go against the traditional model of using discipline.

> I was full of hope when my four-year-old started because he had a diagnosis and an IEP [individualized education program] which included a 1:1, but he was sent to the principal's office all the time and called rude by his aide. He said, "I'm just not good enough for school." My response was "No, kiddo, the school is not good enough for you."

Autism strategies failing

Some schools, including specialist autism placements that claim to be well versed in PDA, insist that standard autism strategies—such as giving direct instructions and sticking to predictable, repetitive routines—will be effective for PDA kids, but they never are. In some cases, rather than changing their approach, schools blame parents for how stressed the PDA child is as a result.

> My son hid from the supposedly autism-affirming therapist and yelled "shut up" at her after she triggered him. Her response was to tell me I need to discipline him.

Expulsion

Without correct support, pressure can cause PDA kids to shout, fight, or otherwise break the school's standards of acceptable behavior. Something has to give, and that's often the school's resolve to keep the child as a pupil.

> My son started in public school in the middle of first grade. He was only attending for an hour a day so that he could "acclimate" to a school setting, which was the administrators' idea. Everyone told me he was doing great, but when it came time for his IEP meeting, I was told that they couldn't accommodate him there any longer because of his behavior. The school changed his placement to a therapeutic day school, which I was OK with, because I wanted him to be successful. As it turns out, even the therapeutic day schools in our area aren't willing to handle his behaviors. He has been sitting at home with me for the entire school year now.

School refusal

Given the multitude of school issues we've so far seen in this chapter, readers might not be surprised to learn that a lot of PDA kids want to avoid going to school. In fact, a survey carried out by the PDA Society in 2018 revealed that 70 percent of young people were not able to tolerate their school environment or were home educated.[6]

> We withdrew our six-year-old from kindergarten in February. She was doing very well academically and seemed to enjoy socializing, but she started refusing school. She would complain of stomach aches every day. She started having panic attacks around library days, to the point of making herself throw up. At home, she would completely lose it and become very aggressive/violent.

Invisible mental health crisis for PDA kids

Internalizing PDA kids can be guaranteed to have intense pressure bubbling beneath their calm facades. Parents talk of PDA kids in high school who respond silently to increasing stress by imploding inward and suffering breakdowns where they can't face leaving home at all.

Please don't read the rest of this paragraph if you wish to avoid being distressed. When the PDA Society ran a survey in 2023, it was revealed that 91 percent of PDA children had experienced severe anxiety, 84 percent had suffered low self-esteem, 70 percent had experienced isolation or loneliness, 52 percent had been depressed, 41 percent had self-harmed, and a horrific 40 percent had had suicidal thoughts.[7] Internalizing PDA can also cause burnout (see Chapter 8).

> Our daughter was diagnosed autistic at age nine, at the exact same time that she noticed girls in her class beginning to actively reject her. She tried to fit in, to no avail, and her sensory triggers seemed to be amplified. She quickly developed psychiatric symptoms, cried often when she got home from school, and began to be fearful and literally begged not to go back.
>
> We unschooled from February to August and then, mistakenly, transferred her to a new school, thinking a solid IEP would be the answer. It wasn't. Our daughter struggled. The light left her. She became fearful again. She hid out in our master bathroom, sitting on the toilet nearly every waking moment she was alone. She said she only felt safe in that bathroom. The school counselor tried to shame me into cracking down on our daughter's school refusal. It was humiliating. And it was so devastating to watch our child suffer like that.

ALTERNATIVES TO MAINSTREAM SCHOOLING

There are many alternatives to mainstream schooling permitted in the USA, which range from chartered partnerships with public schools to completely unenrolling the child. Brook has produced a comprehensive summary of school alternatives in Appendix 1.

> **Brook:** Off and on, I have cycled between being a registered homeschooler in Oregon to enrolling in a homeschool charter. I appreciate that homeschool charters help with education expenses, but sometimes the testing and check-ins get to be too much for either me or my kids. When that happens, I withdraw them to rest and try again later.

TELLING A CHILD ABOUT THEIR PDA DIAGNOSIS

Best PDA practice with regard to how and when to tell a child of their diagnosis differs from what's considered best for autistic kids in general. According to autism best practice, kids must be told about their diagnosis immediately, and not telling them is cruelly negligent because knowing about their autism will help them.[8]

However, unless a PDA kid has actively sought a diagnosis, telling them "You're PDA," or anything similar, is likely to result in them refusing to accept it. This is because PDA brains respond to imposed labels as demands to avoid. Parents of PDA kids have reported their children totally rejecting their diagnosis or initially accepting it but denying it later.

It can pay to broach the general subject, without pressure, when they're in a receptive mood and let them lead. If they're open to hearing about PDA and, for example, the purpose of the assessment they had, it's appropriate to tell them of their diagnosis. Otherwise, it may be better to tell them just a little, such as "The assessors have been wondering about..." or "We're thinking that PDA might fit you. What do you think?" However, in some cases, even the vaguest mention of neurodivergence can trigger panicked resistance. It's best to be sensitive and not push anything.

CHAPTER 8

Adolescence

Content Warning: This chapter "Invisible mental health crisis for PDA kids" mentions self-harm.

Adolescence for all humans is difficult to navigate, but for PDA individuals, it can be harder. The pull towards independence, combined with the need for continued support, creates a unique combination of triggers.

Anonymous quotes are provided by members of an online PDA support group.

SUPPORTING PDA TEENS

Need for direct support in younger years will likely decrease, whereas indirect support will increase. For instance, the child who used to ask you to bring them their food and drink may now feel self-conscious and take on those tasks, but struggle with putting their dishes away and keeping their room clean.

For those children still in public school, education pressures increase. If a child hasn't required an individual education program (plan) (IEP) or 504,[1] this may be the time to add them if the child is comfortable doing so. Young people may need guidance about how to navigate romantic interests with safe and healthy boundaries.

Regardless of how a PDA adolescent's needs have shifted, this is the time to check in while being mindful to offer help only if they wish for it, or if safety is at issue.

For example, dealing with menstruation (periods) is a demand for adolescent girls who may need extra support with hygiene. But parents need to be mindful of how they offer support because, regardless of PDA, teenage girls tend to be highly sensitive about their intimate lives being scrutinized.

If effective PDA support wasn't previously in place, parents can expect a number of struggles, but adopting PDA strategies at any stage will lessen tension and improve family dynamics.

> **Brook:** I struggled (and won) against my mom frequently when I was a young adult. My favorite memory of this was when learning to drive. We took a winding road in the mountains, and I was incredibly triggered by my mom's fears that I was going to cause an accident. It felt like she didn't believe in me, and it pushed me to be even more reckless. I needed her to calmly accept my potential mistakes in order to listen to her guidance.

ISSUES FOR PDA TEENS

It's worth exploring some of the issues that PDA adolescents face. This isn't to say that all PDA teens will have these issues, or that they only crop up at this age. For some kids, issues included in this chapter happen at a younger age; in other cases, they can happen later.

Mental health problems

As we saw in Chapter 7, a high number of PDA kids experience mental health problems, including loneliness and chronic depression. Teenage hormones and other pressures can increase mental imbalance by ramping up our roller-coastering emotions and decimating our self-esteem.

> **Sally:** I was diagnosed with anxiety, depression, and irrational beliefs when I was 19. I was in such a dreadful state of mental health that I thought I was a hideous alien, so being labeled with "anxiety," "depression," and "irrational beliefs" was uplifting because they were things real humans experienced.

Mirrored personality disorders

Potential issues for PDA teens are what we term "defensive borderline" and "defensive narcissism," which resemble borderline and narcissistic personality disorder, but have different internal drivers. For example, a classic narcissist uses gaslighting as a gambit to erode the other person's confidence, but, in mirrored narcissism, gaslighting results from the fantasy adrenal response (see Chapter 3).

We believe these are expressions of extreme emotional dysregulation fueled by teenage hormones double-whammying the already-intense stress load that comes with PDA. Mirrored personality disorders can have a negative impact on both the individual and their families.

Some may object that comparing PDA to personality disorders is unrealistic and will encourage the myth that PDA is an acquired mental illness. But we've repeatedly encountered these high-stress states in the PDA world. Describing proto-personality disorders empowers parents and carers to spot if their PDA kids are using dysfunctional coping mechanisms, as well as giving guidance about how to help, if needed.

Proto-borderline traits are associated with internalized presentations of PDA. A young adult may physically harm themselves as an outlet for their hidden pain. Situational mutism (see Chapter 2) can be a barrier to social interaction which might lead to alcohol and/or substance abuse as a way of overriding our inability to speak.

The social focus that comes with PDA may cause limerence—an all-consuming fixation on a person or persons. We may be unable to directly express our feelings to the object of our desire, or let them go. It can lead to erratic or attention-seeking behavior, and self-perpetuate insecurity when the person we have a crush on rejects or doesn't reciprocate us. Our inability to let go can cause us to put up with toxic relationships.

Proto-narcissism occurs when a PDA youth uses self-centeredness as a coping mechanism for the stress and social anxiety that often accompany PDA. This may manifest as the person claiming they don't care about others or that they're superior to everyone else. As a defense strategy, proto-narcissism is flawed because our sense of superiority is constantly under threat from others surpassing us.

There is no quick fix, but helping a young person to recognize virtues in themselves and in others and to feel comfortable with imperfection can help. Supporting self-esteem through neutral observations and nonjudgmental conversations about narcissism's negative effects may help too. Being candid if a PDA kid upsets you and modeling constructive ways to handle your upset can also be beneficial. PDA and narcissistic traits are also discussed in Chapter 9.

> **Sally:** If I become emotionally dysregulated by my daughter's behavior, I let her know. I may snap, then take time to cool off. When I'm regulated again, I apologize and explain that I can't cope when she's argumentative or disrespectful, but I never stop loving her. When I was a child, my mom used to insist she felt fine when I could clearly sense she was upset, which caused confusion. Had I been inclined that way, her denials might have led me to think I could do no wrong.

Late sleeping

In caricatures, teenagers sleep through mornings after staying up all night. Their behavior is frowned on in Western society, where early rising is prized as a virtue. Sleep is often a big issue for PDA people because sleeping and waking at timely hours triggers our demand avoidance.

On top of this, and regardless of any avoidance, scientific research validates teens' late sleep schedules as something that's dictated by hormones. It's estimated that as many as 16 percent of teens develop delayed sleep phase syndrome (DSPS) because their adolescent hormones interfere with their body's circadian clock, so they sleep and wake much later than the social norm.[2] It's like having jetlag that doesn't reset.

Conventional "wisdom" is that late sleeping is a bad habit that can and should be eliminated via discipline and forcing early starts. Sadly, this works neither for PDA (where discipline backfires) nor for circadian sleep disorders. However, the sleep deprivation that results from stopping kids from catching up on sleep in the morning can have major, negative consequences which include poor grades,[3] an increased risk of serious injuries, substance abuse, mental health problems, and difficulties with self-regulating.[4]

As for PDA in general, we recommend throwing away conventional rule books and thinking of teenagers' late sleeping as something beyond their control, which, as parents, we can best assist by adapting to them instead of expecting them to cease having "difficult" behavior.

Messy bedrooms

Another teen stereotype is messy bedrooms. As for late sleeping, this can be especially common within the adolescent PDA population. This is because PDA-type avoidance is triggered by pressure to tidy up after ourselves (even if the pressure comes from our own aspirations to be a "better" person).

Brook: I was almost always overwhelmed with a messy bed-

> room as a teen. One time, I completely forgot that my mom had someone coming by to clean the house as they did monthly, and my room was especially bad. Instead of leaving my space alone, the house cleaner left a scathing note about how rude I was and gossiped about it with shared friends and family.

Poor hygiene

As for messy bedrooms, so too for personal hygiene: every step of self-care is loaded with demands (go to the bathroom, pick up the toothbrush, put toothpaste on it, run the faucet, etc.). Regular demands for cleanliness are compounded by teen hormones increasing natural body odors and, for AFAB (assigned female at birth) PDA people, there's menstruation to deal with too. The combination of these developmental and regular demands for cleanliness can easily swing into overwhelm and almost complete avoidance. In fact, the more we feel pressured by peers and parents to be clean, the more our demand avoidance against it can escalate.

> **Brook:** Hygiene was another intense struggle for me as a teen. In hindsight, I think if I had someone around to help me understand that it was normal for me to be avoidant and that it didn't make me a "dirty" person, then I would have been able to participate in it more, especially with menstruation.

Violence against siblings and parents

Sadly, it's not uncommon for parents to report violence from PDA teens. It can be helpful to frame this as dysregulation and try to take people/pets out of the room, and when they're calm, coolly troubleshoot what led to it. Triggers may include:

- school
- peer pressure
- diet
- overwhelm
- sensing a parent's dysregulation

- lack of appropriate PDA support.

Remedying the last point (lack of appropriate PDA support) will likely produce the biggest result because it directly counterbalances the stresses that lead to violent reactions.

Some PDA teens are repeatedly violent to their parents, perhaps especially to single moms, who have no parenting support. Because everyone, including parents of PDA kids, has a right to safety, and because enforcing safety can be particularly difficult without causing harm, we recommend organizations like the Alliance Against Seclusion and Restraint as a resource that helps families and schools find alternative ways to address physical violence.

Keep in mind too that enforcing safety is of particular complication for Black, Indigenous, and otherwise marginalized communities of color because of the high risk of death at the hands of law enforcement. Some cities have helped mitigate this by creating local crisis lines where unarmed support can show up to de-escalate mental health crises.

> **Anonymous:** My son's violence started at the onset of puberty and coincided with a lot of external stress factors in our lives. For the next year and a half, we called 911 approximately once a month, sometimes once a week. After two different states' emergency rooms, two child service cases, and many, many pleas for help on my part, we still didn't have any solutions.
>
> I had actually found information about PDA around the time this all started, but it took me everything we experienced to understand, accept, and find the right advice, etc. And then the real work of changing my thinking began, all while I was traumatized and likely PDA myself.
>
> Our life doesn't look anything like I expected it to, but it's a million times better than what it was for everyone involved. I celebrate any success we achieve now. And the longer I give him autonomy to do so, the more my son is slowly coming around to figuring out who he is and what his ambitions are.

People obsessions

The onset of hormones and budding sexuality is a particularly volatile combination when paired with PDA's people focus. Many PDA people report limerence—obsession with another person (see Chapter 1).

We can find ourselves unexpectedly, and helplessly, overwhelmed by an all-consuming crush that takes over our thoughts and ultimately tortures us because we can neither turn our feelings off nor succeed in gaining the intimacy we're craving with the person we're obsessed with. We may be stymied by situational muteness whenever the person we're fixated on is nearby, or we may scare them away by coming on too strong.

Our PDA brains may also develop negative obsessions about people, which cause us to view them as entirely bad, blame them for irrational things and, in some instances, seek to destroy them. This ties in with scapegoating, which is discussed in Chapter 3.

> **Brook:** I had intense fear of romantic relationships in my teenage years, but with an intense, almost obsessive draw toward romantic attraction. This meant it was common for me to pick a person to obsess and fantasize over, but the couple of times that that person became a real possible romantic interest caused me to back away in fear, and burst my fantasy bubble.

Self-harm

As we saw in the last chapter, PDA young people are having an invisible mental health crisis, which includes self-harm. Sadly, unless correct PDA support is put in place, self-harming can carry through into adulthood.

It isn't uncommon for kids who were external in their meltdowns as children to swing over into internalizing their emotions into self-harm. This can be expressed in a number of ways, including unsafe sexual liaisons and misusing alcohol and drugs.

These behaviors resemble emotionally unstable personality disorder (EUPD)—also known as borderline personality disorder—especially if coupled with people obsessions (see above). It's important to work out the root cause of self-harm because standard treatments for personality disorders, such as psychotherapy, may distress an already dysregulated PDA person further. Differences between PDA and BPD are listed in Chapter 4.

Self-harm is of particular risk to kids who weren't supported sooner, so that by the time they hit their teenage years, they have internalized layers of shame and guilt. Once PDA support strategies are in place, the pressure causing their self-harm should reduce.

> **Sally:** I drank vodka and sniffed glue as a young teen. I didn't care about myself at all. My life was unbearable, with the worst pain coming from being a total social loser. Being drunk and high blotted that pain out for a bit.

Rejecting their PDA diagnosis

Aversion to being told what to do is a hallmark trait of any teen, but when you add PDA to the mix, it becomes especially difficult to accept anything that marks us as different from others.

It's considered best practice with autism to be completely transparent with kids during the diagnostic process, because knowledge of their autism helps them understand why they're different. Many parents assume that PDA teens will be equally supported to be told of their diagnosis, but the reality is they're likely to refute it. In fact, at any age, PDA kids and adults may point-blank refuse to accept that they're PDA. This is because our PDA brains register assumptions about us, including diagnostic labels, as demands that must be avoided.

It can be more effective to mention PDA to a teen without categorically telling them that this is what they are, but they may still reject the idea of being PDA; for better or worse, we need to discover things for ourselves to take ownership. It's worth bearing in mind that a teen can be supported with PDA approaches without ever accepting the "why" behind them.

> **Sally:** My intuition told me that I needed to be super sensitive

when telling my daughter about her diagnosis. I told her bits and pieces about PDA and other neurodivergent conditions, traits, etc., when she was receptive. In general, she hasn't wanted to know.

I felt dreadful for years, because my strategy flew in the face of autism best practice. Bit by bit, though, she's wanted to know more, although she hates me mentioning PDA and leaves the room.

What I've done is provide her with the equivalent of a pocket atlas to neurodiversity, which she can consult when, and if, she wishes to.

Not leaving their room

PDA adolescents can spend a lot of time in their rooms because they need much more quiet time than teens do in general. This is because having a constant battle with the demand avoidance our brains hurl at us is exhausting, meaning we need a lot of downtime to recharge. Quiet time is covered in more detail in Chapter 10.

It's important to realize that without extended, unpressured quiet time, we can't self-regulate and will be prone to melting down or burning out.

Sally: My mum complained that my teenage younger brother stayed in his room all the time, playing on his computer instead of being outside playing football like other boys his age. I didn't know about our PDA back then, but I did wonder why she was complaining because instead of running riot, doing potentially risky things, he was fine-tuning a useful skill.

PDA BURNOUT

The extra stresses that bombard PDA youngsters during adolescence can cause burnout, which is a state of physical, mental, and emotional exhaustion. Although burnout causes a person's system to crash as if their battery has gone flat, it differs from ME/chronic fatigue syndrome because it's not a physical disease. Burnt-out people recover their energy if the factors that caused them to burn out are alleviated. Strategies for recovering from burnout are explored in Chapter 10.

FURTHER EDUCATION

Young PDA adults can fare better in further education placements than they did in school because they are treated more as equals by staff and granted autonomy because of this. Other PDA-friendly boons of further education are choice of modules and the novelty of being in a new institution. Further education is easier to cope with than employment for the same reasons, and also because expectations are clearly outlined.

However, once the novelty wears off, demand avoidance is guaranteed to set in, although its strength will vary, depending on a number of factors including how flexible and person-centered the college or university is, the teaching style of individual tutors, and how resilient to demands the young PDA adult is while enrolled.

Demand resilience is dependent on having had enough recharge time to compensate for the demands and other stressors, such as sensory overload, that wear us down. For example, if PDA strategies are used at home, the young PDA person will have energy to tackle the demands of being in college or university. On the other hand, if their home life is stressful, they'll be overloaded and/or burnt out and have no tolerance left for coping with further education.

Many PDA adults give first-hand accounts of dropping out of college or university, but this doesn't have to be viewed as the end of the world. Some of us succeed in completing courses later on in life, and others find good jobs without having gained any qualifications at all.

> **Sally:** I excitedly enrolled on a childcare course after finishing high school, but quickly found myself wanting to avoid it. I switched courses, only to find myself wanting to avoid that one

> too, so I dropped out of college entirely. I enrolled on a different course a year or two later, but dropped out again. Eventually, I succeeded in gaining a bunch of college qualifications.

EMPLOYMENT

Parents frequently raise worries that their PDA teens aren't inclined to work, often adding that their teens just have to because the parents can't afford to support them. Their concerns are merited because our culture frowns on unemployment, and our social system isn't structured to financially support people who can't or won't work. We explore the issue of PDA and employment in detail in the next chapter.

CHAPTER 9

Adulthood

Content Warning: The section in this chapter "Invisible mental health crisis for PDA adults" mentions depression, self-harm, and suicidal thoughts.

It's not unknown for parents and carers of PDA kids to worry when, after becoming adults, their progeny fail to do the things grownups are expected to do. Although some PDA adults manage to live independently, earn a wage, maintain good relationships, and keep themselves and their homes clean, if you've read this far, telling you that many PDA people fail to meet these expectations will come as no surprise. Simply put, the sum total of life's everyday demands is often far beyond our PDA brain's coping ability, and the end result can be epic failure at adulting.

SUPPORTING YOUR PDA CHILD AS AN ADULT

Some PDA children find the transition into adulthood liberating, as their ability to control their life compensates for their demand avoidance, but this is not true for everyone. Supporting an adult PDA child can be challenging for a variety of reasons, including financial dependence, roller-coaster emotions, and poor healthcare.

Financial issues

Financial pressure can cause a lot of friction, because if parents aren't wealthy, funding an adult PDA child can be a struggle. In addition, if PDA isn't understood, parents may resent their adult child's apparent refusal to pay their own way. Western culture has a strong work ethic, meaning there's a lot of prejudice against people who aren't employed, with the assumption being that they're lazy and entitled.

Many parents and carers reach out, saying they can't afford to support their adult PDA kids, so they "must" get a job. Unfortunately, the more a PDA person is expected to work, the more their demand avoidance against working can increase, resulting in a stalemate in which all parties are distressed. We explore employment and disability benefits later in this chapter.

Cohabitation

Another support that adult PDA children may need is permission to carry on living at home. Although Western society expects people to leave home when they reach adulthood, this isn't the case in all cultures, and some have no taboos about adult children continuing to live with their parents until they start a family of their own. In these situations, adult children are expected to contribute to the household, though this doesn't need to be financial. Adults who remain living at home benefit from the extended emotional support that cohabitation and co-regulation bring.

It's a hard fact that there are no easy answers. Regardless of a parent or carer's ability to finance or house them, their adult PDA child may be incapable of supporting themselves or living independently.

> **Brook:** When I started college, I moved in and out of my parents' home a number of times. I remember feeling the need to be close to them, and trying to ignore the judgment of others for having this need, but it made me feel safer knowing that I could live at home as I needed to.

Emotional support

PDA adults are pretty much guaranteed to be emotionally dysregulated because of the roller-coaster nature of our emotions. One benefit from transitioning into adulthood is that parents may find it easier to treat their adult children as equals. The resulting equalized relationship may enable an adult PDA child to be open about their struggles and ask for guidance.

> **Brook:** It drove me crazy as a kid that so few adults in my life talked to me like I was capable of understanding their thinking. Once I was an adult, I saw that it was a little easier for my family, my mom especially, to be more open with me, and by extension, it was then easier for me to be open with them. Of course, my mom is still my mom, and from time to time, I have to remind her that I need her to allow me space to make choices, even if this leads to making a mistake.

Healthcare

We PDA adults often struggle with healthcare, both in terms of looking after our body's needs and with regard to attending medical appointments. This can cause us to have escalating chronic and/or acute health problems. To make matters worse, in our experience, neurodivergent people are particularly prone to illness and may react badly to medicines that are fine for most people.

The issues PDA adults face with healthcare shouldn't be disregarded. Without support, our demand avoidance against seeking timely medical intervention and sticking to vital treatment plans has been known to cut PDA people's lives short.

We tend to respond badly to well-meant advice about improving our health, because it triggers our demand avoidance. We may, though, be receptive to a general discussion about the pros and cons of healthier habits. We may also respond better to a parent's, or other person's, concern for our health if they take ownership of the worry they're feeling and respect that we might not want to be preached to. For example, someone telling us, "You have to take better care of your teeth" will go down less well than them saying, "I'm personally worried about your dental hygiene, which is the reason that I'm mentioning it, but I also realize that you might not want to discuss it. Would it be OK for me to tell you what's worrying me?"

We may be more appreciative of assistance with making and attending healthcare appointments. For example, many PDA people have high demand avoidance against phone calls and will be relieved if someone offers to phone a doctor on their behalf. Some of us may also find it easier to attend appointments if someone we trust goes along with us. However, it's important not to presume that help is wanted and to offer it rather than impose it.

> **Sally:** A tragic example of the issues PDA people have with healthcare played out in an adult PDA online community a few years ago. One of the friends I made was hospitalized with pneumonia because she'd avoided seeing her GP when she became so ill from a cold that she struggled to breathe. Her husband found her unconscious and called an ambulance. She was diagnosed with pneumonia. She kept missing outpatient appointments because of demand avoidance against attending them. She pleaded for us to persuade her to get out of her car and go into the hospital. It breaks my heart, but the pneumonia, which would have been treated successfully, beat her in the end, and she's no longer with us.

Granting responsibility

PDA adults can feel empowered if people trust them to take responsibility for things. This might sound contradictory because, surely, the crux of the problem is that parents, and society, want PDA adults to pay their own way and live independently.

What PDA adults may actually need is to have our inability to meet life's standard goals acknowledged, accepted, and supported without judgment, and, beyond this, to be treated as worthy and capable of accomplishing some things.

Regardless of what issues might arise, we PDA people are more likely to flourish if we don't feel scrutinized or judged. When given support, space, and freedom to find our own ways forward, we can, and do, achieve amazing things. See Chapter 5 for a summary of PDA positives.

> **Sally:** It was in my early 20s that I realized my bid to rid myself of all responsibilities, though successful, had failed to make me happy or fulfilled, and that the few, rare responsibilities I'd been trusted with were lifting me up in a vital way. The responsibilities in question were creative opportunities that I didn't feel pressured into doing, such as being loaned an expensive video camera as part of a free course.
>
> The most empowering responsibility I'd been granted was producing artwork and writing leaflets for a local drugs and alcohol peer education charity. I loved being appreciated and being able to help other people.

INVISIBLE MENTAL HEALTH CRISIS FOR PDA ADULTS

The results of a mental health survey published by the PDA Society in 2025 (which we visited in Chapter 7) reveal that PDA adults reported even worse mental ill-health problems than their younger counterparts:

- 96 percent suffered severe anxiety
- 93 percent had low self-esteem
- 90 percent experienced isolation or loneliness
- 83 percent had been depressed
- 66 percent had suicidal thoughts
- 60 percent had self-harmed.[1]

These figures confirm what adult PDA people express in peer groups, and what we have experienced ourselves. Although we don't retract what we've said about PDA positives (see Chapter 5), we're very aware that PDA can simultaneously curse us with massive mental distress. For example, our sensitization to adrenal reactions can mirror personality disorder and compound PTSD (see Chapter 4).

ABUSE AND VULNERABILITY TO ABUSE

One of the negatives associated with PDA is abuse, which can go either way, because although PDA people may be abusive to others, they may also be the recipients of abuse.

Unintentional abuse

Harm doesn't have to be intentional for it to count as abuse. And it can go both ways. For example, if a parent or carer tells their adult PDA child to stop using demand avoidance as an "excuse" and get a job like everyone else, this doesn't make their demand avoidance go away, but instead crushes their self-esteem and makes them feel like a total failure. We've previously seen that PDA adults are experiencing an invisible mental health crisis, and attacks to our self-esteem can be truly catastrophic.

Similarly, a PDA person may subject a loved one to emotional abuse during a meltdown. Although they're not in control of what they're saying and doing at this time, the impact on the recipient can be devastating.

Another common issue is misunderstandings and damaged relationships when two neurodivergent people have different communication styles. For instance, although PDA people are currently categorized as a subgroup of autism, the typical autistic preferences for direct, clear, and unambiguous communication can actually trigger PDA rejection sensitivities. A mediator or therapist may be required to help formulate guidelines for finding methods of communication that feel safe and clear for both people.

It should be borne in mind that PDA people are particularly prone to experiencing unintended abuse because of our naturally high anxiety and "trigger-happy" adrenal glands. This can be especially problematic if a person close to us, such as a parent, doesn't use PDA strategies, so that demand pressure and anxiety keep building.

> **Brook:** I lacked role models growing up to show me how to repair relationships. They used words but not actions, and that disconnect made it very confusing for me to navigate the conflicts that occur naturally in relationships, and set me up for abusive dynamics.

Forms of abuse

Although people may tend to think of abuse as physical or sexual, abuse can also be emotional or the result of neglect. Examples of emotional abuse are constant criticism, shouting threats, ridiculing, forcing the victim to degrade themself, scapegoating and gaslighting (see below), and emotional neglect resulting from someone we're dependent upon, such as a parent or spouse, dismissing our feelings or being unable to handle them—for example, snapping, "You're too sensitive!" because they're already exhausted from dealing with other things, so their child's sensitivity feels too much to accommodate.

Scapegoating

If, in place of seeking empathy, we let our frustrations escalate, we can end up scapegoating family members for imagined crimes. We saw in Chapter 3 that many PDA adults say their parents scapegoated them, and that this type of blaming behavior appears to be the result of diverting adrenal "F" defense responses into fantasy, by which fear and self-doubt are alleviated by fantasized certainty that our bad feelings are someone else's fault. In some instances, scapegoating may be caused by a PDA person developing a negative obsession about someone else (see Chapter 1).

Although scapegoating might make us feel better in the short term, it can make things much worse overall and corrode peace. To give an example, if an adult PDA kid blames their mom or dad for everything that's wrong in their life, their fantasized victimization will stop them finding ways to make the most of who they are, despite any limitations. Similarly, if a parent treats their adult PDA kid as someone who's ruining their life, this will cause their kid to be more dysregulated, so the cycle of strained family relationships continues.

Gaslighting

Gaslighting means pushing someone to believe that their perception of reality is wrong, so they mistrust their own judgment. It's similar to scapegoating because it passes the buck of responsibility to somebody else.

A PDA person might gaslight their family by, for example, insisting that they'd never agreed to help with the garden or pay towards rent. The PDA person's gaslighting may be aided by charm or bubbling outrage that makes them seem very convincing.

Conversely, when an adult PDA child asks a parent or carer if they're angry, they might deny it because they want to protect their child's feelings, or if feeling harassed, they might snap, "I didn't mean it like that!" Although these scenarios might not seem like abuse because the parents or carers aren't trying to inflict harm, telling someone that their perception is wrong invalidates their self-trust and teaches them to dismiss self-protective instincts and let others treat them badly. This can be especially devastating if the person being gaslit has low self-esteem (see the section "Invisible mental health crisis for PDA adults" above).

Protective narcissism

Both scapegoating and gaslighting are behaviors associated with narcissistic personality disorder (NPD). However, in the cases described above, the PDA individuals aren't attempting to manipulate others. Instead, they are using narcissistic-type traits as maladaptive coping mechanisms for dealing with the anxiety, roller-coaster emotions, and social confusion that commonly come with PDA.

This isn't to say that their effect on others is any less damaging. It can be helpful to understand why a PDA person is behaving in a narcissistic manner, and that there may be no sinister agenda behind their confusing behaviors. The differences between PDA and NPD are discussed in Chapter 4, and defensive narcissism is discussed in Chapter 8 in the section "Mirrored personality disorders."

> **Brook:** Toward the end of my marriage, my partner was in crisis, and it was common for them to try to minimize my reactions to the trauma. In part, it was my PDA that helped keep me out of being gaslit because I sensed the manipulation, but my fixation with my partner made me vulnerable to believing their reality.

Taking responsibility to stop abusing others

From a PDA adult's perspective, our PDA doesn't give us a license to hurt others without making an effort not to repeat that harm. We may not be in control during a meltdown, but it is within our control to learn what triggers us and avoid repeating circumstances that have previously led to a meltdown.

If, for example, hunger makes us irritable and prone to meltdown, it's our responsibility to avoid repeat triggers by, for example, eating, taking time out, or warning others away. Saying "I'm PDA, so you have to put up with whatever I throw at you" isn't OK. But a parent or carer saying "You are evil because of your meltdown" isn't OK either. Everyone deserves respect, regardless of their neurology, and regardless of whether their role is that of child or parent/guardian.

It's helpful for parents and carers of PDA kids to realize that if we become angry or upset with a loved one, it's better to admit to it, instead of scapegoating them for our hurt, or gaslighting them that it didn't happen. By explaining why we lost it and the ways we plan to avoid revisiting triggering circumstances, we reassure our adult PDA children that the stress they sensed in us wasn't their fault. As a bonus, this provides them with a working model for dealing with their own emotional overwhelm constructively.

> **Sally:** I've learned to be wary of people who never apologize. This isn't because I want them to grovel or fawn, but because it's a sign that they don't take responsibility for their actions, meaning they're likely to do the same thing again and again.

Vulnerability to grooming

A fair few PDA adults, including us (Sally and Brook), have fallen victim to groomers who've manipulated us into ceding our own needs in favor of theirs. Our vulnerability to grooming may stem from a combination of PDA traits:

- social naivety (see Chapter 1)
- social equalizing drive, which may compel us to rescue an abuser who's pretending to be weak, wounded, and downtrodden (see Chapter 5)
- negative people obsessions, which can be exploited by groomers to turn against people who have influence over us (see Chapter 1)
- loneliness and low self-esteem, which may make us easy pickings for predatory abusers who use charm and pretend to be our new best buddy (see earlier in this chapter)
- the fawn "F" adrenaline response (see Chapter 3)
- imposed masking (see Chapter 2).

It can be monumentally hard to steer a PDA person from a manipulator's influence because our demand avoidance makes us actively resist guidance. It may be more effective to hold back from intervening and, instead, be unjudging and unswervingly welcoming. We PDA people need to work things out for ourselves, and we're more likely to protect our own needs if we're not pressured to do so.

> **Brook:** It has always been a struggle for me not to get into manipulative dynamics. For starters, I never saw how to speak out for my needs clearly, so I didn't know how it was done. Then, add to that how my neurodivergence means that I struggle with strongly feeling the emotions of others as if they are my own, and that there is a painful demand in showing anyone how I really feel, because who knows how complicated the fallout could be? People-pleasing was my master strategy for many years and almost killed me.

ALIENATION FROM FAMILIES

Alienation from one or more close family members is all too often recounted in adult PDA forums. It can be the result of a family member severing all contact with us, or of us instigating the break, or a combination of both. Factor in PDA running in families, but with no awareness of PDA, and there's a perfect storm for dysfunctional dynamics to run rampant.

Breakdowns of family relationships can be painful and distressing, perhaps especially for PDA people, with our emotional sensitivity and need to both feel in control and to have safe co-regulators near at hand. The most effective strategy may be to accept things without seeking to change them. The resulting lack of pressure can enable the stressed PDA relative to calm down and then, in their own time, be drawn back to their family by their natural bond.

> **Sally:** A PDA person I'm close to had a brother who was so dominating and undermining that she had an emotional breakdown against engaging with him at all. On top of this, her younger brother has stopped communicating with her. Her father freaked the family out with his meltdowns until her mum kicked him out, and, last but not least, she broke off all

communication with her mum after a therapist helped her realize that she couldn't move forward while her mother was constantly undermining her. My friend is sure all these family members are undiagnosed PDA.

EMPLOYMENT AND PDA

Our society values gainful employment above just about everything else, but few PDA people seem to be able to embrace this vibe. Just as for school, being an employee entails a barrage of unremitting demands, including fixed hours, dress codes, and the expectation that orders will be obeyed without question.

Western culture is structured in a particularly non-PDA-affirming way. On the one hand, workers are expected to cope independently, while, on the other hand, the work ethos is unnecessarily cutthroat. Self-made success is lauded, and the worker-bee mentality is rewarded. All of this is very confusing for PDA people to navigate, because while we thrive when we are independent in our pursuits, we also do best with equitable professional affiliations.

Sally Cat's peer comparison study[2] included eight employment-specific traits, of which six scored significantly more highly for PDA than for the general autistic population:

- I can't cope with being told what to do by bosses and managers.
- I am not motivated by money, but will work for hours unpaid so long as there is no demand that I do this.
- I can't cope with deadlines.
- I can't cope with being confined to a workplace.
- I can't cope with being an employee unless given a lot of authority and/or autonomy.
- I can't cope with tax returns.

Some PDA people get on better with freelancing or self-employment, although both options entail the demand of perpetually seeking new jobs. And then there's the demand-horror of tax returns.

If working for an employer, PDA people may fare better if their role feels meaningful. It might also be worthwhile seeking employers with inclusive policies who offer flexi-time and remote working. However, no matter how many accommodations are in place, being an employee always entails the demands of servitude and compliance that challenge PDA people.

> **Sally:** When I was self-employed as a pub quiz master, I found it really hard to write two new quizzes every week. It was like the force you feel when you try to push same-pole magnets together. It was really hard to overcome it.

Disability benefits

Disability benefits can be a lifeline for PDA adults. The sobering reality is that a large number of us aren't able to work to earn livable incomes. We've met too many fellow PDA adults who've been driven by the resulting poverty to petty crime or become homeless.

Applying for benefits is a process of intense scrutiny that assumes that those applying are lying or not "bad enough" to receive help. The process is difficult for everyone, but it is especially difficult for PDA people for a number of reasons, such as an aversion to being observed, having an instinct to mask our struggles, and a need for sufficient appointments with qualified professionals who can back up our claims.

It can be helpful to find someone to help with applications, because the process can be so stressful that many PDA people give up. Disability attorneys don't take an up-front fee but receive a portion of back pay from their successful cases.

> **Brook:** I didn't know it was PDA burnout that I was going through in my late 20s. All I knew was that I couldn't function. The reality was that I was disabled from that point for the next

ten years, but all the hoops we are required to jump through for disability to validate me made it impossible for me to receive benefits.

CHAPTER 10

Effective Strategies and Interventions

In this final chapter, we explore strategies and interventions that have a good track record of effectiveness for PDA people, young and old. Although many people presume that the best way to fix problem behaviors, such as meltdowns and burnout, is through medication, implementing PDA strategies may generate better results by alleviating the root causes. Preempting triggers can be thought of as erecting a fence along a dangerous cliff edge, as opposed to parking an ambulance at the bottom.

PDA strategies

The first base for remedying stress with PDA is implementing effective strategies. The term "PDA strategies" is often used in parent/carer forums to mean imposing zero demands on PDA kids. But as we'll see, attempting to apply zero demands is neither practical nor helpful.

Our PDA strategies comprise several, distinct PDA-appropriate tactics whose relevance varies according to the situation. The strategies we've included differ from standard lists, because we've added candor (being open) and empathy, which are person-centered techniques that we believe are vital to restoring and maintaining harmony in PDA relationships. We've created the "DANCER" acronym to make it easier to remember the full set: Deflection, Anxiety reduction, Negotiation, Candor, Empathy, Reducing demands.

Deflection

Using humor, distraction, and/or role play may divert a PDA child or adult's escalating stress before it skyrockets. It's important to do this in a respectful, open way. Attempting to "trick" a PDA person into thinking about something else will likely backfire. Sensing that someone is trying to manipulate us can generate massive demand avoidance and damage trust.

Genuine humor, on the other hand, may signal safety in reminding everyone that not every situation is as serious as it initially seems. Role play might serve as a buffer by putting us in a land of pretend where we have more imagined control.

Anxiety reduction

Being prone to anxiety is a core PDA trait (see Chapter 1). It's impossible to buffer us from becoming anxious, because countless things can trigger it. But it is possible to reduce the number of anxiety triggers that confront us.

Effective techniques for minimizing anxiety include finding strategies to calm ourselves, keeping the PDA individual informed of what's going on (uncertainty can overwhelm us), but not over-preparing them (too much preparation can feel like pressure), and front-loading success by removing known anxiety triggers from future plans. For example, if a PDA child is panicked by crowds, it might be worthwhile planning a vacation in a more secluded place.

Negotiation

Offering choice and involving PDA people in decision making enables us to maintain that vital sense of personal control (see Chapter 1). Negotiating could be thought of as the opposite of imposing demands.

But beware: having too many choices can ignite our demand avoidance! It might be most effective to offer two or three simple choices, in a low-key way—for example, "Would you like pasta or noodles for dinner?"—or not using language at all and setting out options with a gesture if conversation is too triggering. It also helps to be accepting if the PDA person responds with a third option you hadn't even suggested!

Candor

Some carers of PDA kids try to shield them if they get stressed by putting on a smile and acting as if they're just fine. Although this incongruence (emotion hiding) is meant benevolently, it may inadvertently distress the child. PDA people tend to be super sensitive to other people's moods, even if we're poor at communicating it, so if a significant other insists that they're fine when we can clearly sense that they're not, our imaginations may panic about what they're hiding.

Not being candid also runs the risk of undermining the PDA person's self-confidence (see the section on gaslighting in Chapter 9). It tends to be more effective if stressed-out family members are honest about their feelings and take time out. Then, once they've calmed down, they can apologize if they snapped at the PDA person and use the conflict as an opportunity to model that we are all flawed, by explaining how all humans lose their temper sometimes. After all, authentic examples from carers is the least demanding and most meaningful way to help PDA children learn how to moderate their own roller-coaster emotions.

Empathy

Compassionate empathy, cognitive empathy, and emotional empathy are three different ways people can walk in someone else's shoes. Not every person has access to all three kinds of empathy, but, at its core, the purpose of empathy is to limit assumptions that we know what another is feeling, and to value how it can pay dividends to genuinely consider their perspective in a nonjudgmental way.

It is all too easy to assume erratic PDA behaviors are rooted in selfishness or deliberate trouble-making. However, as we saw in Chapter 2, PDA is an invisible condition, and its drivers are therefore hidden from view.

Realizing that a "tantrum-ing" child is in anxiety overload will guide us to resolve their distress in an effective and compassionate way. Similarly, understanding that playing the clown and telling fibs are adrenal responses (see Chapter 3) enables us to see beyond surface-level dysfunctional behavior. Feeling understood unlocks the best potential for connection with PDA people, while feeling misunderstood only builds up higher walls and escalates behavior issues.

Reducing demands

Reducing demands means limiting them but not removing them completely. This is because it's not possible to remove all demands from anyone's life. Our PDA brains are also primed to interpret anything and everything as a demand, even our own body's signals.

Although we can't prevent a PDA child's body from signaling demands like thirst, hunger, and the need to pee, it's possible to reduce the quantity of external (non-bodily) demands. This could include permitting a child to leave the dinner table early, or letting them dress as they please.

It's still important to establish and maintain boundaries. Although boundaries are demands, some are 100 percent necessary, and this is where the concept of "picking our battles" comes into play. We're more likely to make the effort to push through our demand avoidance if we're given more choices in other areas to compensate for those areas where compromise isn't an option. Examples of non-negotiable boundaries are road safety, nonviolence, and hygiene (which many families have to temporarily limit or drop during burnout, as discussed below in the "Low-demand or low-pressure parenting" section).

Summary of PDA strategies

It might help to think of these individual PDA strategies as playing cards that can be laid down singly or in combination, depending on the situation. For example, if a PDA child is burnt out from demand overload, reducing demands might be the most appropriate strategy. If, on the other hand, a panicked PDA child has started fibbing, it might be better to combine empathy, anxiety reduction, and negotiation to defuse their dysregulation. If a desired task is tackling triggering, implementing humor or role play might make the task feel less threatening.

STANDARD ACCOMMODATIONS

Low-demand or low-pressure parenting

Low-demand approaches require assessing what's truly important based on immediate circumstances. The low-demand approach tends to be most relevant if a PDA person is in crisis. The phrase "low-demand parenting" was coined by the online PDA parenting community prior to the publication of Amanda Diekman's book of the same name in 2023.[1] The concept of low demand applies to adapting parenting expectations to support PDA children, but can also be applied to PDA adults struggling with burnout.

The goal of low demand is to give back as much control as possible to a PDA person to help them heal from an overall lifestyle that previously deprived them of sufficient personal control. For parenting, low demand might look like asking:

- "Is it really important that you use your child's energy by pressuring them to sit at the table to eat dinner with the family?"
- "Is working with your school leading to stress, instead of progress?"
- "Can you afford to keep your child home to recover?"
- "Can you drop some of the limits on screen time so that they feel they have more control over regulating themselves when stressed?"

With adults, low demand gets more complicated because we are typically responsible for housing and feeding ourselves, and we might also have children to care for. It's not uncommon for exhausted PDA adults to be caring for exhausted PDA children. It can be challenging to negotiate which appointments are essential, what kind of work suits us best when we're struggling to leave the home, or whether or not it's best to let the housework go.

It is worth noting that what each individual can afford to let go will be different based on what resources and privileges they have to support them during a crisis. Stressors generated from failing to fit mainstream expectations may vary according to race, religion, and culture.

In the long term, applying low-demand strategies should shift us out of the mindset of pushing ourselves and our families to match our concept of "typical." It should give us permission to use a discerning eye about what priorities uniquely fit our needs. When it comes to parenting, the idea is to reserve your child's energy for what they are actually able to achieve, so they can grow into an adult who is energized and able to find a future that suits their strengths.

> **Brook:** I experienced two major burnouts, the first of which meant my spouse and I had to move out of our home and move back in with my parents while I was taking care of a newborn and parenting a two-year-old. Ten years later, I feel less anxious and guilty when pressures get too high for me to maintain my home or when I suddenly feel too drained to keep up with

appointments. Experience teaches me that it is best to remove or adjust my life stresses first, and worry about appearances later.

Ross Greene's collaborative parenting solutions

Dr. Ross Greene's popular book *The Explosive Child* proposes that instead of viewing childhood problem behaviors through the lens of "How do I get them to comply?" we should reframe most behaviors as communicating overwhelm, and that, as a rule, "Kids do well when they can."[2]

The CPS (collaborative parenting solutions) model, outlined in Greene's book, asks parents to put their expectations of their children into three categories:

- Plan A: desires we have for our children that don't involve their input, and that they are, for the most part, able and willing to achieve.
- Plan B: things that adults collaborate with children on, in order to involve them in decision making.
- Plan C: things kids are not able to work on currently because their energy is being used on other, more important skills or tasks.[3]

The CPS model was not written for any specific diagnosis, but does suit PDA needs particularly well. This is because the collaborative component in Plan B harmonizes with PDA people's essential need to have an element of personal control. In fact "low demand," as described in the section above, can be seen as a natural extension of implementing the CPS method for PDA-specific struggles. One particular hurdle with using CPS for PDA is that PDA kids will commonly struggle to answer the questions outlined in Greene's book.

Our next section goes further into discussing how language itself presents invisible triggers for PDA kids. For now, it's maybe worth making a simple note that direct questioning isn't always the best way to collaborate with PDA children.

Declarative language

Many PDA people are involuntarily triggered by language containing hidden demands—imperatives such as "You have to..." and even "I hope you will..." Kindly meant advice like "You should rest now" or "You'll love this film" can feel demanding because of the implied expectations that we should agree with someone else's assessment of the situation or thing.

Using declarative language may bypass these demand triggers. *The Declarative Language Handbook*, authored by speech and language pathologist Linda Murphy,[4] outlines speech patterns which may remove some of the demands that are nested within language itself. Think of declarative statements as someone making observations out loud to neutrally share thoughts, opinions, and feelings.

Example:

> Imperative: "Put your shoes on, it's time to go." (Loaded with urgency and offers no choices to the receiver.)

As opposed to:

> Declarative, indirect: "I'm getting ready to leave." (By focusing on the speaker's behavior, the phrasing implies a gentle, unpressured invitation for the participant to join in.)

Also:

> Declarative, direct: "I would like us to go soon. If so, we need our shoes." (This communicates the adult's desire to leave, and gives clarity about what the next logical step is, but is phrased in a way that invites consent, instead of assuming it.) There are nuances and ways to adapt declarative language to each situation—for example, by using fewer words if complex instructions are too demanding to process, or by incorporating body language to help signal the next logical steps in a task.

Declarative language is not meant to bypass demand avoidance and should not be used to manipulate children into complying with specific outcomes. However, declarative language may help resolve some deadlocks. For example, if a child insists on leaving the house barefoot, by using declarative language, caregivers can pack shoes to be available if the child becomes uncomfortable walking barefoot. As long as basic safety is observed, the declarative language approach can enable harmonious decision making, even if its outcomes are unexpected.

THERAPIES

As mentioned at the beginning of this chapter, it is common for families to assume that therapy is the solution for all PDA struggles. While each family has unique needs, PDA on its own does not require therapy. In fact, demand loads from therapeutic settings can easily cancel out any potential benefits. Appointment times, discomfort from feeling observed, and meeting therapy goals can escalate demand pressure. Because of this, we advise parents and carers to embark on therapy in place of their children. The more adult carers understand PDA and heal their own traumas, the better equipped they are to create a safe environment for their children to thrive in.

If families choose to seek therapy for PDA children, there are a few adaptations for reducing pressure:

- Steering toward trauma-informed, play-based, and relationship-based approaches and away from behavior-based therapy.
- Allowing time for a relationship to develop between the child and practitioner before expecting participation.
- For older ages, finding practitioners who offer flexible platforms, like Zoom, so that appointments can take place at home.
- Spreading out appointments to allow for longer rest periods between sessions.

- Screening for PDA-aware professionals who do not suggest typical autism support (such as applied behavior analysis).
- Remembering that most therapies rise or fall based on the professional who is implementing them. An otherwise decent therapy can be ruined by a practitioner who is too demanding, while a less appropriate-seeming therapy can be helpful if offered by a compassionate, flexible practitioner.
- Finally, recognizing there is no perfect therapeutic approach and being on the lookout for signs of stress that indicate the effort is costing more than the results ("Is the juice worth the squeeze?").

MEDICATION

Medication should always be overseen by a medical professional. It can, at times, change a family's life, but we caution that families should be prepared that finding the correct medication can be a long-term process of trial and error. It is also worth mentioning that no amount of medication can or should compensate for prioritizing lifestyle adjustments.

As with any intervention, success with medication hinges not only on finding the correct one(s), but on the PDA person's engagement with taking it. Forcing or hiding medication in food breaks trust, so we never recommend doing so. It is better to invite the PDA individual into the process, starting with building a rapport with the professional who oversees medication management and explaining how medication might help and what outcome they might expect.

Remember, there is no medication "for" PDA, and every person's makeup is unique, so a provider will be focusing on alleviating co-occurring conditions, such as anxiety and depression. PDA people can be extremely sensitive to side-effects and interactions with other medications, so it can be helpful to keep a record of what you try and any side-effects you notice.

NUTRITIONAL SUPPLEMENTS AND ALLERGIES

A common topic in PDA parent and carer forums is PDA emotional tolerance being impacted by nutritional deficiencies and food sensitivities. While we hold the position that nothing causes PDA, and it cannot be cured, some physicians will run tests screening for deficiencies or allergies that might be impacting overall wellness. For instance, MTHFR gene variants (which can be tested for) impact the body's ability to process folate, increasing the risk of heart disease, stroke, depression, and anxiety.[5] Also, some parents notice increased emotional dysregulation after their children eat artificial food colorings, dairy, or wheat. Avoidant/restrictive food intake disorder (ARFID) seems to be extremely common in PDA families (see Chapter 4). If a child's food intake is restricted, it may be more important for them to eat *anything*, regardless of nutritional value.

If you are planning to change a PDA child's diet, it's important to gain their consent. Otherwise, the changes you bring in will be interpreted as demands. It's worth emphasizing that food should not be turned into a battleground.

IN CONCLUSION

Harmonious relationships with PDA folks are achieved when approached from multiple angles. First priorities are to adjust demands and build equitable and safe relationships that will support PDA people lifelong. It takes time to see positive changes. Most families are in crisis by the time they hear about PDA, meaning children and families have accumulated trauma and/or have complex medical needs that cannot be fixed overnight.

When learning about PDA, it can be beneficial to connect with local and online resources to help the natural feelings of isolation, depression, and discouragement that go with being an atypical family.

"BUT HOW WILL THEY PREPARE FOR THE REAL WORLD?"

This has to be one of the most frequently asked questions people raise when they understand what supporting PDA entails. Hand in hand with this are real concerns about "enabling" someone who appears capable in one moment and arbitrarily incapable the next.

Based on our insiders' point of view, we remind readers that PDA is a real though hidden disability. The insight and advice we have gathered here is pulled from our personal lives in raising PDA children, our own trauma recovery from lives spent as unsupported PDA adults, and the combined voices of others who identify with PDA, either personally or as carers.

Our collective journey has been one of seeking answers without finding any diagnoses that properly guided treatment, "failing" at life despite searching for help, and ultimately finding affirmation, mutual support, and a growing pool of shared wisdom in the worldwide PDA community. This is what we hope we offered with this book.

APPENDIX 1

Alternatives to Mainstream Schooling

The USA has a complex variety of alternatives to mainstream schooling, which are summarized below.

In-person charter schools

Charter schools are funded by public dollars but are structured differently based on their "charter"—a unique, written document that lists students' rights and privileges. Charters are not always the best option for kids who require flexibility as the school can be pressured to test and document student performance to justify their existence to the state.

Private schools

Private schools don't face the same kind of oversight that charters do. Their difficulty is expense; they are typically not funded by government dollars, and only families who can afford their fees can choose this as an option.

IEP school placement

All students are entitled to FAPE (free and appropriate public education) and that sometimes means that a student is placed in an alternative school with government dollars. The journey to accessing this can be difficult as public schools may push back if their perception of a student's needs doesn't match the parent's.

An individual education program (plan) (IEP) advocate can be an invaluable resource if pursuing this route.

School-at-home

It used to be that school-at-home brought to mind religious zealots or fearful parents who didn't want to expose their children to alternative ideas, but since the Covid-19 pandemic, families and public schools alike have learned that schooling from home or offering flexible alternatives is an asset to many.

School-at-home differs from homeschooling because the curriculum is controlled by a public school. Although many people refer to school-at-home as homeschooling, technically homeschooling is when you unenroll from public school.

Homeschool charters

These are charters that partner with families who still want access to teachers and funding. They are varied in structure, from the more lax ones that let you choose your own curriculum and only ask for periodic check-ins, to the more rigid ones that provide a specific online program. Legally, a homeschool charter is still considered public school as it is funded by federal and state dollars, has the same requirements and opt-outs for state testing, and offers a diploma at completion.

Charters from home are an increasingly attractive option as the more flexible ones can be almost completely adapted to the child's needs. Keep in mind, though, that the structured charters can present the same triggers to PDA children unless you have an IEP. As stated above, acquiring an IEP from a charter can be difficult.

There are some homeschool charters that are offered nationwide, and some only offered state by state, so it's worth connecting with local homeschooling and charter school communities.

Registered homeschooling

Withdrawing a child from public school entirely to educate from home with minimal government oversight is called "registered homeschooling." Registered homeschooling laws vary state by state. Some states don't track registered homeschoolers at all, some ask for periodic testing, and others require portfolios with yearly check-ins. Families should research and connect with other local homeschoolers to decide if it is a fit for them.

Traditional homeschooling

Traditional homeschoolers are those who rely on curriculum, whether online modules or book format. It typically follows a structure, even if it paces itself based on the child's skills. This style of homeschooling doesn't always work for PDA children without some adaptation. The personalized element and control need of PDA usually means that the curriculum will need to be adapted to avoid triggering PDA anxiety that leads to burnout.

Unschooling

Unschooling is merely a style of schooling from home that is structured to follow the child's interests and can be done if you are a registered homeschooler or attending a homeschool charter that is relaxed enough to allow for it.

Radical unschooling eschews curriculum entirely and trusts that children will learn the relevant information they need to succeed in life simply by being allowed to follow their natural curiosity. Many families follow a hybrid of unschooling and traditional homeschooling. These are families who opt to use a curriculum on occasion or for certain subjects, but otherwise let their child lead or use their child's interests to branch off into other subjects. This flexible structure can work for many PDA families.

Glossary

504	provides disability supports for students to access mainstream education settings (e.g., an ADHD child having a quiet room to take tests in to limit distractions)
AAC	augmented and alternative communication
ABA	applied behavior analysis
ADD	attention deficit disorder
ADHD	attention deficit hyperactivity disorder
AFAB	assigned female at birth
Alexithymia	being unable to identify or describe our own emotions. Sometimes termed "emotion blindness"
ARFID	avoidant/restrictive food intake disorder
ASWD	advanced sleep-wake phase disorder
AuDHD	autism and ADHD combined
BIPOC	Black, Indigenous, (and) people of color
BPD	borderline personality disorder
CSDs	circadian sleep disorders
CPS	collaborative parenting solutions

CPTSD	complex post-traumatic stress disorder
DSPS	delayed sleep phase syndrome
dyssy	dyslexia, dyspraxia, dyscalculia, and dysgraphia
EHCP	education, health, and care plan (UK)
EDA	extreme demand avoidance
EDA-Q	Extreme Demand Avoidance Questionnaire
EDS	Ehlers–Danlos syndromes
EUPD	emotionally unstable personality disorder
FAPE	free and appropriate public education
FII	fabricated or induced illness
GAD	generalized anxiety disorder
GP	general practitioner
IEP	individual education program ("plan" in the UK)
Limerence	an intense, often unreciprocated, positive obsession about a person
MCAS	mast cell activation syndrome
Non-24	non-24 sleep-wake disorder
NPD	narcissistic personality disorder
NVLD	nonverbal learning disorder (NVLD)
OCD	obsessive-compulsive disorder
ODD	oppositional defiant disorder
PANDAS	pediatric autoimmune neuropsychiatric disorders associated with streptococcal infections
PANS	pediatric acute-onset neuropsychiatric syndrome

PBIS	positive behavioral interventions and supports
PDA	“pathological” demand avoidance
PTSD	post-traumatic stress disorder
RSD	rejection sensitive dysphoria
Spare play	playing alongside other children to hide solo play from observers
SPD	sensory processing disorder
Synesthesia	experiencing senses through unrelated sense organs (e.g., hearing an object’s color)

Endnotes

Introduction

1 Collins Dictionary (2025) Pathologize. www.collinsdictionary.com/dictionary/english/pathologize

2 Kushner, H.I. (2017) Stuttering and "retraining" left-handed children in mid-century U.S. Johns Hopkins University Press News. www.press.jhu.edu/newsroom/stuttering-and-retraining-left-handed-children-mid-century-us

Chapter 1

1 The Newcastle upon Tyne Hospitals NHS Foundation Trust (2023) Understanding and supporting the social interaction of autistic children and young people. www.newcastle-hospitals.nhs.uk/resources/understanding-and-supporting-the-social-interaction-of-autistic-children-and-young-people

Chapter 2

1 Kupferstein, H. (2018) Evidence of increased PTSD symptoms in autistics exposed to applied behavior analysis. *Advances in Autism* 4, 1. http://dx.doi.org/10.1108/AIA-08-2017-0016

2 van Baaren, R., Janssen, L., Chartrand, T.L., and Dijksterhuis, A. (2009) Where is the love? The social aspects of mimicry. *Philosophical Transactions of the Royal Society B Biological Sciences* 364, 1528, 2381–2389. https://doi.org/10.1098/rstb.2009.0057

3 Sally Cat PDA (2023) Peer research insights into PDA. www.sallycatpda.co.uk/2023/03/peer-research-insights-into-pda.html

4 Grand Valley Animal Hospital (2025) Pet pain—why animals hide it and what you can do to help. https://grandvalleyvet.com/pet-pain-why-animals-hide-it-and-what-you-can-do-to-help

5 Sally Cat PDA (2022) Internalised PDA – the quieter, but equally impactful presentation of PDA that's hard for people to spot. www.sallycatpda.co.uk/2022/04/internalised-pda-quieter-but-equally.html

Chapter 3

1 O'Nions, E., Christie, P., Gould, J., Viding, E., and Happé, F. (2014) Development of the "Extreme Demand Avoidance Questionnaire" (EDA-Q): Preliminary observations on a trait measure for pathological demand avoidance. *Journal of Child Psychology and Psychiatry* 55, 7, 758–768. https://doi.org/10.1111/jcpp.12149

2 Walker, P. (2003) Codependency, trauma and the fawn response. Pete-Walker.com. https://pete-walker.com/codependencyFawnResponse.htm

3 Rape Crisis England & Wales (n.d.) The 5Fs: fight, flight, freeze, flop and friend. https://rapecrisis.org.uk/get-help/tools-for-victims-and-survivors/understanding-your-response/fight-or-flight/

4 Hassall, M. and Hunter, B. (2005) Fight, flight, freeze...or fib? *ADDitude*, 9 May. www.additudemag.com/why-lie-adhd-fight-flight-freeze.

5 See note 1.

6 Bagnall, R., Russell, A., Brosnan, M., and Maras, K. (2021) Deceptive behaviour in autism: A scoping review. *Autism 26*, 2, 293–307. https://www.ncbi.nlm.nih.gov/pmc/articles/PMC8814957

7 Sally Cat PDA (2022) Internalised PDA – the quieter, but equally impactful presentation of PDA that's hard for people to spot. www.sallycatpda.co.uk/2022/04/internalised-pda-quieter-but-equally.html

8 See note 1.

9 Spiegel, D. (2024) What are dissociative disorders? American Psychiatric Association. www.psychiatry.org/patients-families/dissociative-disorders/what-are-dissociative-disorders

10 Porges, S. (1995) Orienting in a defensive world: Mammalian modifications of our evolutionary heritage: A Polyvagal Theory. *Psychophysiology* 32, 4, 301–318.

11 Dana, D. (2024) The science of feeling safe enough to fall in love with life. Deb Dana Rhythm of Regulation. www.rhythmofregulation.com/polyvagal-theory

Chapter 4

1 Cat, S. (2022) *Sleep Misfits: The Reality of Delayed Sleep Phase Syndrome & Non-24*. Independently published.

2 Sally Cat PDA (2024) A comparative study of PDA and non-PDA autism: Exploring distinctive traits in adults. www.sallycatpda.co.uk/2024/10/a-comparative-study-of-pda-and-non-pda.html

3 Rydzewska, E. (2016) Unexpected changes of itinerary—adaptive functioning difficulties in daily transitions for adults with autism spectrum disorder. *European Journal of Special Needs Education* 31, 3, 330–343. https://doi.org/10.1080/08856257.2016.1187889

4 McElroy, R. (2015) PDA—is there another explanation? British Psychological Society. www.bps.org.uk/psychologist/pda-there-another-explanation

5 Children's Hospital of Philadelphia (2019) Brain imaging shows how minimally verbal and nonverbal children with autism have slow response to sounds. Press release, September 17. www.chop.edu/news/brain-imaging-shows-how-minimally-verbal-and-nonverbal-children-autism-have-slower-response

6 Lovering, N. (2022) What to know about nonspeaking autism. PsychCentral. https://psychcentral.com/autism/autism-nonverbal

7 The Guild for Human Services (2021) Ask the expert: "nonspeaking" vs. "nonverbal" and why language matters. www.guildhumanservices.org/blog/ask-expert-nonspeaking-vs-nonverbal-and-why-language-matters

8 American Psychiatric Association (2013) *The Diagnostic and Statistical Manual of Mental Disorders*, 5th edition (DSM-5). Washington, DC: APA.

9 ARFID Awareness UK (2025) What is ARFID? www.arfidawarenessuk.org/what-is-arfid

10 ARFID Awareness UK (2025) ARFID and autism. www.arfidawarenessuk.org/the-link-with-autism-1

11 See note 1.

12 Circadian Sleep Disorders Network. www.circadiansleepdisorders.org

13 *See note 1.*

14 The Ehler–Danlos Society (2025) What is EDS? www.Ehlers–Danlos.com/what-is-eds

15 Dellwoo, A. (2025) What's the difference between chronic fatigue syndrome and fibromyalgia? Verywell Health. www.verywellhealth.com/chronic-fatigue-syndrome-vs-fibromyalgia-5213420

16 WebMD Editorial Contributors (2023) What is hyperlexia? www.webmd.com/children/what-is-hyperlexia

17 In the US, "learning disabilities" is used to denote the "dyssy" conditions (e.g., dyslexia); these are termed "learning difficulties" in the UK (see below).

18 Foundation for People with Learning Difficulties (2025) Learning difficulties. www.learningdisabilities.org.uk/learning-disabilities/a-to-z/l/learning-difficulties

19 BMJ Best Practice (2025) Assessment of learning difficulty and cognitive delay. https://bestpractice.bmj.com/topics/en-gb/884

20 Adina ABA (n.d.) In-depth guide to profound autism symptoms. www.adinaaba.com/post/profound-autism-symptoms

21 Autistica (n.d.) Learning disability and autism. www.autistica.org.uk/what-is-autism/learning-disability-and-autism

22 Mast Cell Action (2025) About MCAS. www.mastcellaction.org/about-mcas

23 See note 22.

24 Mayo Clinic Staff (2023) Obsessive-compulsive disorder (OCD). Mayo Clinic. www.mayoclinic.org/diseases-conditions/obsessive-compulsive-disorder/symptoms-causes/syc-20354432

25 Cleveland Clinic (2022) Rejection sensitive dysphoria (RSD). https://my.clevelandclinic.org/health/diseases/24099-rejection-sensitive-dysphoria-rsd

26 See note 25.

27 Cleveland Clinic (2025) Sensory processing disorder. https://my.clevelandclinic.org/health/diseases/sensory-processing-disorder-spd

28 Cleveland Clinic (2023) Synesthesia. https://my.clevelandclinic.org/health/symptoms/24995-synesthesia

29 National Institute for Neurological Disorders and Stroke (2025) Tourette syndrome. www.ninds.nih.gov/health-information/disorders/tourette-syndrome

30 Hartmann, A., Szejko, N., Mol Debes, N., Cavanna, A.E., and Müller-Vahl, K. (2021) Is Tourette syndrome a rare condition? *F1000Research 10*, 434. https://doi.org/10.12688/f1000research.53134.2

31 ADDA Editorial Team (2023). DSM-5 criteria for ADHD: How is adult ADHD evaluated? Attention Deficit Disorder Association. https://add.org/adhd-dsm-5-criteria

32 Cleveland Clinic (2023) Emotional dysregulation. https://my.clevelandclinic.org/health/symptoms/25065-emotional-dysregulation

33 Sally Cat PDA (2023) The Polyvagal Theory and PDA. https://www.pdasociety.org.uk/what-is-pda/what-if-its-not-pda/

34 Watts, R. (2022) Fabricated or induced illness (FII) and perplexing presentations—New guidance for social work practitioners. Special Needs Jungle. www.specialneedsjungle.com/fabricated-or-induced-illness-fii-and-perplexing-presentations-new-guidance-for-social-work-practitioners/#FII_accusations_harm_families

35 Mayo Clinic Staff (2017) Generalized anxiety disorder. Mayo Clinic. www.mayoclinic.org/diseases-conditions/generalized-anxiety-disorder/symptoms-causes/syc-20360803

36 Miller, C. (2025) What is nonverbal learning disorder (NVLD)? Child Mind Institute. https://childmind.org/article/what-is-non-verbal-learning-disorder

37 Cleveland Clinic (2022) Oppositional defiant disorder (ODD). https://my.clevelandclinic.org/health/diseases/9905-oppositional-defiant-disorder

38 Mayo Clinic Staff (2024) Borderline personality disorder. Mayo Clinic. www.mayoclinic.org/diseases-conditions/borderline-personality-disorder/symptoms-causes/syc-20370237

39 Hall, J.L. (2022) 8 types of children scapegoated in narcissistic families. Psychology Today. www.psychologytoday.com/gb/blog/the-narcissist-in-your-life/202202/8-types-of-children-scapegoated-in-narcissistic-families

40 Mayo Clinic Staff (2024) Separation anxiety disorder. Mayo Clinic. www.mayoclinic.org/diseases-conditions/separation-anxiety-disorder/symptoms-causes/syc-20377455

Chapter 5

1 Stuart, L., Grahame, V., Honey, E., and Freeston, M. (2019) Intolerance of uncertainty and anxiety as explanatory frameworks for extreme demand avoidance in children and adolescents. *Child and Adolescent Mental Health* 25, 2, 59–67. https://doi.org/10.1111/camh.12336

2 Sally Cat PDA (2024) A comparative study of PDA and non-PDA autism: Exploring distinctive traits in adults. www.sallycatpda.co.uk/2024/10/a-comparative-study-of-pda-and-non-pda.html

Chapter 6

1 O'Nions, E. and Eaton, J. (2020) Extreme/"pathological" demand avoidance: An overview. *Paediatrics and Child Health* 30, 12, 411–415. https://doi.org/10.1016/j.paed.2020.09.002

2 Egan, V., Linenberg, O., and O'Nions, E. (2018) The measurement of adult pathological demand avoidance traits. *Journal of Autism and Developmental Disorders* 49, 481–494. https://doi.org/10.1007/s10803-018-3722-7

3 Good2Know Network (2023) Early identity formation: How children develop a sense of self. https://good2knownetwork.org/early-identity-formation-how-children-develop-a-sense-of-self

4 Ball, C. (2023) Making memories matters, even if your baby won't remember them. Parents.com. www.parents.com/kids/development/childhood-amnesia-heres-why-your-child-cant-remember-being-a-baby

5 Smith, B. (2021) Time-space synaesthesia: How some people perceive the "shape" of days, weeks and years. ABC Science. www.abc.net.au/news/science/2021-12-13/time-space-synaesthesia-psychology-cognition-spatial-calendar/100677210

Chapter 7

1 PDA Society (2022) Identifying and assessing PDA. www.pdasociety.org.uk/what-is-pda-menu/identifying-assessing-pda

2 Sally Cat PDA (2024) A comparative study of PDA and non-PDA autism: Exploring distinctive traits in adults. www.sallycatpda.co.uk/2024/10/a-comparative-study-of-pda-and-non-pda.html

3 O'Nions, E., Christie, P., Gould, J., Viding, E., and Happé, F. (2014) Development of the "Extreme Demand Avoidance Questionnaire" (EDA-Q): Preliminary observations on a trait measure for pathological demand avoidance. *Journal of Child Psychology and Psychiatry* 55, 7, 758_768. https://doi.org/10.1111/jcpp.12149

4 Anthony, M. (n.d.) The social and emotional lives of 8- to 10-year-olds. Scholastic Parent & Family Blog. www.scholastic.com/parents/family-life/social-emotional-learning/development-milestones/emotional-lives-8-10-year-olds.html

5 Fidler, R. and Daunt, J. (2021) *Being Julia: A Personal Account of Living with Pathological Demand Avoidance*. London: Jessica Kingsley Publishers.

6 PDA Society (2025) PDA lives worth living. www.pdasociety.org.uk/wp-content/uploads/2025/05/PDA-Society-PDA-Lives-Worth-Living-Report.pdf

7 See note 6.

8 Oredipe, T., Kofner, B., Riccio, A., Cage, E., *et al.* (2023) Does learning you are autistic at a younger age lead to better adult outcomes? A participatory exploration of the perspectives of autistic university students. *Autism* 27, 1, 200–212. https://doi.org/10.1177/13623613221086700

Chapter 8

1 A 504 provides disability supports for students to access mainstream education settings (e.g., an ADHD child having a quiet room to take tests in to limit distractions). It is a less stringent process than an IEP. For more, see: Rise Educational Advocacy (2025) IEP vs 504 Plan: Understand the difference and choose right. www.riseeducationaladvocacy.com/blog/iep-vs-504-plan?

2 Cleveland Clinic (2023) Delayed sleep phase syndrome. https://my.clevelandclinic.org/health/diseases/14295-delayed-sleep-phase-syndrome-dsps-in-children-and-adolescents

3 Richter, R. (2015) Among teens, sleep deprivation an epidemic. Stanford Medicine News Center. https://med.stanford.edu/news/all-news/2015/10/among-teens-sleep-deprivation-an-epidemic.html

4 Garey, J. (2024) Teens and sleep: The cost of sleep deprivation. Child Mind Institute. https://childmind.org/article/happens-teenagers-dont-get-enough-sleep

Chapter 9

1 PDA Society (2025) PDA lives worth living. www.pdasociety.org.uk/wp-content/uploads/2025/05/PDA-Society-PDA-Lives-Worth-Living-Report.pdf

2 Sally Cat PDA (2024) A comparative study of PDA and non-PDA autism: Exploring distinctive traits in adults. www.sallycatpda.co.uk/2024/10/a-comparative-study-of-pda-and-non-pda.html

Chapter 10

1 Diekman, A. (2023) *Low-Demand Parenting: Dropping Demands, Restoring Calm and Finding Connection with Your Uniquely Wired Child.* London: Jessica Kingsley Publishers.

2 Greene, R.W. (2021) *The Explosive Child, Sixth Edition: A New Approach for Understanding and Parenting Easily Frustrated, Chronically Inflexible Children.* New York, NY: Harper.

3 See note 2, p.42.

4 Murphy, L.K. (2020) *The Declarative Language Handbook: Using a Thoughtful Language Style to Help Kids with Social Learning Challenges Feel Competent, Connected, and Understood.* Self-published.

5 CDC (2025) MTHFR gene variant and folic acid facts. www.cdc.gov/folic-acid/data-research/mthfr/index.html